DISCARD

Wreaths&Bouquets

PAULA PRYKE
Wreaths&Bouquets

Photography by SARAH CUTTLE

RIZZOLI
NEW YORK

In memory of Ivan Bussens and Juliet Clarke
for their joy, talents and friendship

First published in the United States
of America in 2008 by
Rizzoli International Publications, Inc.
300 Park Avenue South
New York, NY 10010
www.rizzoliusa.com

Originally published in the United Kingdom
in 2008
as *Seasonal Wreaths & Bouquets* by
Jacqui Small LLP,
7 Greenland Street
London NW1 0ND

Text copyright © Paula Pryke 2008
Photography, design, and layout copyright
© Jacqui Small 2008

Publisher **Jacqui Small**
Editorial Manager **Lesley Felce**
Designer **Maggie Town**
Editor **Sian Parkhouse**
Production **Peter Colley**

2008 2009 2010 2011

10 9 8 7 6 5 4 3 2 1

ISBN: 978-0-8478-3086-2

Library of Congress Control Number:
2008927577

Printed in Singapore

contents

introduction

This is my twelfth flower-arranging book, and this one concentrates on the two most common styles of flower arrangements that we use in our home decoration: Bouquets, which hopefully we receive, and which we also regularly display in our home, and wreaths, which most of us like to have as decoration at least once a year, and increasingly more often.

When I was first approached by my American publisher to write a book about wreaths and bouquets, I did not really think that they went very well together! However, when I started to think about them seasonally, I realized how the seasons affect the way we see and use materials and, whatever design we are aiming at, the seasonality of the material will dominate the design.

Obviously, in today's global economy and with plants and flowers being shipped all over the world, the idea of seasons being strictly adhered to has largely been eroded. Having said that, it is interesting how our natural desires move towards seasonal items and, in particular, our desires for certain colors do follow quite a strict seasonal palette. In the spring, I am desperate to use a little yellow, whereas for most of the year I could happily live without it, and I do not care so much for it except again in late summer when I am drawn to sunflowers and dill. In the summer, I return again and again to my favorite pinks, purples, and blues, and in the autumn I want a bit of passionate color to brighten up my short dark days. Winter is a time for appreciating the foliages and for making the most of seedheads as well as dried fruits and nuts. The bounty of winter is not as generous as that of summer, but it allows us to be more creative and to appreciate the foliage that surrounds us all the year round. Variegated foliage, for example, which I also care little for the rest of the time, can be a godsend in a grouped evergreen wreath at Christmas!

In this book, I have set out to give some inspiration as to how to use seasonal flowers in your homes, both as hanging decorations and as table arrangements, and as little gifts for friends and relatives. Whatever your level of skill, I hope there is something to inspire or admire and you find arrangements in this book that you can enjoy at home whatever the season.

Happy Arranging!

spring

spring
inspirations

**I FIND THE SEASON OF SPRING A GREAT JOY, AS THE RARE AND TREASURED
SEASONAL CROPS START TO APPEAR IN THE FLOWER MARKETS**

After months of dormant ground and days upon days of working with the sort of
highly cultivated flowers that are available all year, we begin to witness the rising of
the sap in the trees and bushes and the movement of bulbs in the cold earth. By the
time Valentine's Day is over we are able to choose from a tantalizing array of spring
bulb and tuber production, and also some fantastic early foliages and blossoms.
Bundles of glorious forced peach blossom from Italy, wrapped in green cotton, is the
first commercial blossom to arrive, and then for two months until the end of April I
find that my designs are inspired by the branches, bulbs, and mosses of the season.

   Spring can be a mass of seasonal color, but nature is a great designer and so the
early season dictates the use of pale yellows and creams and also the soft blues of
iris and Muscari, through to the deep blues of the viola and hyacinth families. In midspring yellow is prominent, when this less fashionable color takes the central stage for
a short burst! The grayness of the season and the cold and the damp make this color
very welcome at this time of year. Then as the spring warms up you start to get
some new foliage and some wonderful blossoms on trees, such as the white apple
blossom, the early gray-green foliage of *Sorbus*, or the blossom from the viburnum
family, most notably the green balls of *Viburnum opulus*. This is the best time for
scented branches, with the trailing sprigs of *Genista* and taller branches of mimosa
from the south of France and Italy being my favorite.

For me, spring is the season of the
garden flowers, when I am inspired
by all the emerging growth outdoors to
create beautiful arrangements indoors.
Violets, snowflakes, muscari, iris,
narcissi, hyacinths, freesias, willow,
alder, and camellia are just a few of
my favorite spring cuts.

The wonder of spring is the re-birth of nature, and all the pleasure that brings to the flower lover and designer. This scented spring bouquet of lilac, guelder rose, daffodils, mimosa, freesia, ranunculus, and tulips ('Negrita' and 'Madison Garden') is a tightly packed bundle of delight to me.

what spring
means to me

As the weather warms I find spring draws me outdoors and fills me with new hopes for my garden. Spring is the beginning of the gardening year, and as the frosts cease the borders start to stir again. I never cease to be impressed by the sudden re-appearance of a plant that has been buried for the whole of winter, or the sprouting of leaves and flowers from branches that have been dormant for months.

Spring for the florist is always a very busy time. No sooner have you cleared away all the trimmings of Christmas than you become focussed on Valentine's Day, making bows and bags and preparing the wrapping for all the bouquets that will be sold in just a few short hours on the eve of St. Valentine and on the big day. Following shortly on from that is Easter, with Mother's Day not long after. There are two themes that are central to my designs for the spring; one is the use of a lot more planted material such as bulbs and the use of lots of small plants with fresh moss. The cheap costs of bulbs and the selection of lots of diminutive plants at this time of year ensure they appear in most of our contracts, gift work, and even in some of our events at this time of year. The second focus is on branches, with the sap rising in the bushes and trees, and this is demonstrated in the pages that follow. The young branches of pussy willow, *Prunus*, japonica, and dogwood are soft and pliable at this time, and they are used to fashion wreaths, as mechanics in vases, and as part of the form of many arrangements.

tulip time

THE TULIP, THAT MOST SYMBOLIC OF SPRING BLOOMS, HAS A FASCINATING HISTORY AND IS CENTRAL TO ANY STORY ABOUT THE FLOWER INDUSTRY

It is documented that on a crisp and clear fall day an elderly botanist called Carolus Clusius planted a handful of tulip bulbs in a small garden in Leiden in the Netherlands, and this event is considered by the Dutch as the birth of their famous flower industry. Although Carolus was interested in the medicinal qualities of the tulips bulb, he had been cross-breeding bulbs for some years and had acquired these bulbs in Vienna, although they are likely to have originated in the Ottoman Empire, which had enjoyed a golden age in the sixteenth century. Carolus had previously been Head of the Medicinal Garden in Vienna and had been given some bulbs and seeds from the Austrian Ambassador to the Ottoman Emperor. In 1593, no Dutchman had ever seen a tulip flower in Holland, but in the next 400 years they were to became so synonymous with Holland that one would imagine that they were native!

A frenzy ensued over these exotic beauties, and fortunes were lost and won. In a wildly speculative marketplace, the bulb traders were the equivalent of today's hedge fund managers. Prized single bulbs were sold for more than you could get for one of the smartest canal houses in Amsterdam, complete with servants and carriages! Although the bubble burst in the spring of 1637, the attraction while it lasted for these bulbs was for their hugely individual patterns and colors and the potential for cross-breeding and creating new varieties. It is because of the tremendous hybridization of tulips that they are still one of the world's favorite flowers.

left A packed bouquet of multicolored tulips nestles snugly in a tall cylinder vase encircled by a wreath of prunus stems secured with twists of red wire. The fresh green buds on the bare branches are a hint of growth to come.

opposite There is a a wonderful sense of movement to this wreath, with the green stems and leaves of 'White Dream' tulips and 'Black Eyed Beauty' calla lilies swirling among dark prunus.

this page 'Garnet Glow' calla lilies, ranunculus, 'Blue Heron' tulips, and real quails' eggs that have been blown and then stuck carefully in place with a hot glue gun, decorate a bonnet formed from pliant birch stems.

right A combination of birch and willow branches, with their dangling catkins and soft sprouting buds, have been twisted and woven into a basket-shaped wreath encircling a bouquet of 'Blue Diamond' tulips.

tulip nests

There has to be a tulip for everyone's taste, from the simplest white to the flamboyant striped parrot of the later season. Their immense variety, beauty, and versatility mean that they look great in minimal designs, country styles, or even grandiose classical arrangements. Brightly colored assemblies are great for kids' parties, bar mitzvahs, or simple arrangements. The cool, subtle-colored tulips look great in contemporary interiors, while the deeper colors and the fancy varieties compete with opulent traditional interiors. They are the *crème de la crème* of spring bulbs, affordable, long lasting, with lots of new cultivars being introduced each year. In the United Kingdom the Royal Horticultural Society gives a merit award to plants that are

excellent and reliable, and so far a staggering 181 awards have been make to tulips, which gives you some idea just how many varieties are cultivated each year! I am very drawn to the tulips from the Fringed Group, which is one of the newest and only recognized in 1981. The crystalline ends of the petals are astounding; they flower in May in my garden but can be found in the flower markets from February to May. The first frilly-edged tulips to be grown successfully as a commercial cut flowers was the yellow variety known as 'Fancy Frills'. At that time a double yellow variety know as 'Monte Carlo' was the biggest selling cut tulip and yellow was very popular, though currently the fashion for yellow has declined.

spring bouquets

THESE ARE PERFECT FOR SHOWCASING SPRING FLOWERS, HIGHLIGHTING THEIR DELICACY OF FORM

Bulbs harvested as cut flowers are relatively inexpensive, and so the spring is the perfect time to arrange flowers and experiment with new designs. Spring flowers are also the best to try your hand at making your first hand-tied bunches, and great for getting used to spiraling flowers in your hand. Narcissi, tulips, and hyacinths are grown in huge numbers in a myriad of varieties, and they are all short with little foliage on their stems, which makes them easy to handle. Other favorites at this time of year are the jewel-colored anemones, and my number one all-time favorite flower, ranunculus. When selecting a collection of material for a bouquet, I always try to include foliage or flowers that give movement to the design. The catkins and lysimachia give a wild, natural effect in the small bouquet (right), while the long ivy trails encircling the massed bouquet (above) give that a more natural feel of movement.

this page The sharpness of this combination of *Hellebore argutifolius*, 'Dutch Master' daffodils, alder catkins, veronica, lysimachia, margarita daisies, and yellow ranunculus, with its glowing yellows and almost acidic greens, is wonderfully refreshing at the beginning of the season.

this page This tightly massed bouquet of 'Cheerfulness' narcissi is spiraled and hand-tied, and the stems are cut level so that they stand up without support. It has been embellished with orange raffia held in place with pearl-edged trim. Using a single variety of flower is a much cleaner backdrop for the almost mesh-like design of the overlay.

this page A sense of energy bursting through is suggested in this tight mass of plump buds and unfurling flowers. A bouquet of peony tulips, scented *Mahonia aquifolium*, ranunculus, yellow *Narcissus* 'Dick Wilden,' and cream *Narcissus* 'Geranium' with an orange center, sits in a gray woven basket.

you will need

- 100 stems of *Muscari* 'Bluefields Beauty'
- 5 bunches of *Viola pyrenaica*
- 3 bunches of *Narcissus* 'Carlton'
- 3 bunches of *Narcissi* 'Geranium'
- 5 bunches of snowflake (*Leucojum aestivum*)
- a roll of green string
- a wreath-shaped clear glass bowl

1 Clean all the stems of any additional leaves or foliage. Divide the different flower varieties into seven equal bunches. Taking a central flower from the first bunch in your left hand, gradually add flowers at right angles to the central flower until you have placed about five stems, and then twist.

2 Add another five flowers, and then twist again. Continue twisting in sections like this until you have added all the flowers. Trim all the flowers to one length to make it easier to handle. For this design we cut the stems to about 2⅕ inches long.

3 Tie firmly just under the flower heads, but take care not to damage the fragile stems by tying too tightly. Place the bunches around the glass ring so that they are equally spaced in the vase and form a circle.

pretty bouquet bowl

TINY BOUQUETS SUCH AS THESE LOOK GREAT
INDIVIDUALLY AND EVEN NICER GROUPED IN A RING

potted rings

WORKING WITH PLANTED MATERIALS IS ALWAYS FUN— RATHER LIKE BEING A GARDEN DESIGNER IN MINIATURE

Spring bulbs and plants are inexpensive, and so placing them together in an arrangement with some moss is a great way of making an affordable long-lasting centerpiece. Before starting your design, it is always a great idea to give the plants and bulbs a long drink—just as you would if you were going to plant them in your garden. You can anchor plants into wreaths or arrangements by using heavy stub wires and placing them into the soil or, if the plants are really heavy, insert a bamboo cane through the base.

this page A plastic-backed floral foam ring has been decorated with cut prunus stems and planted with *Narcissus*, hyacinth bulbs, and primrose plants. The wreath has been trimmed with moss and decorated with chicken and quails' eggs, all encircling a glass fish bowl filled with floating candles.

this page A mossed wreath has been decorated with primroses, blue hyacinths, and *Narcissus* bulbs. A few twisted stems of *Corylus* and the odd catkin have been worked through the wreath to add movement.

you will need

- a 14-inch wreath frame
- a selection of bulb plants (I have used *Muscari* and hyacinths)
- some leaves from the *Tillandsia* plant
- some small-leaved succulent plants (I used *Pachyphytum*)
- a selection of miniature terracotta pots
- sphagnum and bun moss
- a selection of heavy stub wires
- a florist's knife

1 Soak the wreath frame until the air bubbles cease to rise. Trim the edges of the wreath to make it more rounded and natural.

2 Cover the foam by pinning in handfuls of the moss and then wiring in the plant material, working in a clockwise direction around the wreath. Remove the earth from the bulbs that are going to be placed without a pot and tease out the roots. Wire in the terracotta pots by placing a wire through the hole in the base.

3 Continue around the wreath, placing plants in different directions to create a growing effect. Fill in any gaps with moss and then pin in the *Tillandsia* leaves.

indoor spring garden

THIS SCULPTURAL PLANTED WREATH RELIES ON SHADES
OF GREEN AND FANTASTIC TEXTURES FOR ITS EFFECT

Easter decorating

EASTER IS THE TIME FOR SPRING HOLIDAYS, A TIME FOR RELAXING AND ENTERTAINING

Traditionally the oldest and the most important Christian festival, Easter is the celebration of the death and the resurrection of Jesus Christ. For Christians this represents a new beginning, following the solemnity and abstinence of the 40 days of Lent. It is the highlight of the calendar for flower arrangers, as all churches are decorated fully with spring flowers usually in white, cream, or yellow, and traditionally including lilies. Although Easter is a Christian festival, it is derived from the Jewish festival of Passover and pagan rituals celebrating spring and fertility in particular, focusing on eggs and rabbits, which have been documented by the first historians. Its commercial and marketing opportunities seem to have begun in the U.S., but with mass globilization there

seems to be a fusion of traditions and ideas, with an egg hunt after the Easter Bunny has been. There are individual traditions: in England this involves bread buns with the sign of the cross on them—known as hot cross buns—and simnel cake. In parts of Scandinavia it is more common to make decorations with painted eggs, and it is customary for children to dress up and collect candy in exchange for decorated pussy willow. On Sunday a smorgasbord with smoked fish follows. In the Netherlands, tables are laid with painted eggs and decorated with spring flowers and plants. In some northern European countries they light bonfires as a symbol of the end of winter and to kill any bad feelings that have occurred over the long winter season.

left The versatility of wreaths means that they work equally well when laid flat as a table decoration as they do hung on a wall. This natural-feeling spring wreath has been created by filling a glass dish with willow twigs and then threading ranunculus and tulips through the framework. The bowl is filled with water to keep the whole thing fresh.

opposite A mossed wreath has been decorated with hummocks of bun moss, hazel, ranunculus, and calla lilies. Some white plastic eggs and real quails' eggs have been glued directly onto the wreath using a hot-glue gun.

left Bright yellow napkins are trimmed with small bouquets of *Muscari* tied with decorative lime-green ribbon.

opposite To create this sumptuous design you will need one large floral foam ring, blue emu eggs, a selection of chicken eggs, the very darkest anemone ('Meron Bordeaux'), bunches of *Narcissus*, plus guelder rose, mimosa, freesias, *Muscari* 'Bluefields Beauty,' sphagnum moss, and a few stems of *Corylus avellana* 'Contorta.'

below A cut-open emu egg has been secured into the foam base and then filled with a bouquet of spring flowers.

the Easter table

The egg as the symbol of fertility and the fragility of life is central to Easter celebrations. The last few weeks of winter would have been very lean times for our ancestors; there was not much in the way of food growing in the frozen fields, and livestock did not have any milk for human consumption until after their own young were weaned. Even hens could not be relied upon for regular egg production until the 1930s, when farmers learned how to coop them up in pens so that they would be encouraged to lay. It is no wonder then that when the buds finally started to open that a celebration was in order.

I like to include real eggs in my easter decorations, and large emu or ostrich eggs as well as quails' and regular chicken eggs are now also sold alongside flowers and plants at the huge Dutch auctions. If you are using eggs for the table, it is advisable to give them a good wash before you add them to decorations.

The most famous decorative eggs were make by the Russian jeweller Carl Fabergé for the Czar Alexander III of Russia as an Easter surprise for his wife, Maria. The empress was so impressed with the gift that Fabergé was appointed the court supplier and went on to produce many more. The ornate eggs opened up to reveal jewels and were reminiscent of the way Russian dolls open to reveal more treasures inside. The over-the-top egg table center for an Easter lunch shown here is inspired by those highly decorative jeweled eggs.

you will need

- a basket (I have used a birch basket that has been flocked)
- a plastic pot
- a bag of woodslice
- a box of blown hens' eggs
- some small feathered cockerels on picks
- a hot-glue gun
- 20 stems of double green and red ranunculus
- 30 stems of yellow ranunculus
- 30 stems of *Hypericum androsaemum* 'Cream Classic'

1 Insert the plastic pot into the center of the basket. Decorate the birch twig base of the basket with small handfuls of woodslice (a by-product of the wood industry that can be bought in natural or colored form from florist and hobby suppliers), eggs, and the wired feathered birds. The woodslice can be pushed in among the twigs, while the blown eggs will need to be wired in place using the strings attached to them.

2 Clean the stems of the ranunculus and hypericum, trimming off all foliage, and spiral into a tightly packed bouquet.

3 Fill the plastic pot with flower food mixed with water. Trim the bouquet to fit inside it, and finish by adding more birds and woodslice through the bouquet to create a harmonious effect between the bouquet and the base.

eggs and chickens

COMBINING A HAND-TIED BOUQUET
AND A WREATH BASKET CREATES
A TABLE CENTER OF GREAT DEPTH
AND INTEREST

seasonal napkin ideas

Not so long ago an upscale restaurant or hotel would demonstrate the skill of its wait staff by exhibiting the art of the folded napkin. This may take the form of a swan, a butterfly, or even the design for the Sydney opera house! However, this artifice required the sort of voluminous highly starched heavy linen napkins that few of us possess or have the energy to launder! So, for both informal and formal parties, the recent trend has been to trim simpler cotton napkins with flowers, herbs, and ribbons. This makes the table look more decorative and is an easy way to embellish a simple event. It allows you to introduce a temporary color to the table for that event and has the bonus that the decorations can be detached and taken home by your guests at the end of the meal.

My favorite spring flowers to use on flat napkins are calla lilies or elegant tulips. A long stemmed freesia also makes a great addition and introduces a fabulous scent to the table. However, my favorite if I have the time is to pip some hyacinths and wire together the heads to make a natural napkin ring.

left Pussy willow is now available for many weeks of the year and the extended season begins well before Christmas and goes on to June. There are also some very pretty commercially grown new varieties of pussy willow that vary from lime green to deep gray. Here I've combined a few lengths with long-stemmed 'Silver Dollar' tulips in a very simple wired bouquet.

opposite, top left This sumptuous bouquet of velvety purple anemones is studded with individual wired hyacinth pips and tied with a purple bow.

opposite, top right For me this yellow-themed bouquet is the very essence of spring: prunus blossom, mimosa, and primroses are tied with a green ribbon.

opposite, bottom left Cool and simple, the green centers of the snowdrops echo the fresh grassy shade of the napkin, and the posy is tied with raffia.

opposite, bottom right A twisted hazel napkin ring holds ivy berries and leaves, cupping peach Parrot 'Blondine' tulips.

Using flowers as napkin trims is a great way of coordinating your table

Spring flowers twisted into bouquets or fixed to mini-wreaths that loop around the napkin itself, lend themselves wonderfully to this type of small-scale design, as you can really appreciate the beauty of the individual flower heads. Repeat the design or make each napkin ring a personal treat.

I love Mother's Day because the young visitors to my shops are instinctively drawn to the scents and colors of the flowers. They are encouraged to make their own choices, to choose their bow and wrap, and so enter into the creative experience of buying flowers. This delightful hand-tied bouquet of *Cytisus*, *Viburnum opulus*, 'Jan Bos' hyacinths, and 'Blenda' tulips, all swathed in pink tissue, will definitely make someone's day!

Mother's Day

WHOSE MOTHER WOULD NOT BE THRILLED TO RECEIVE A SUMPTUOUS BOUQUET PACKED WITH SPRING FLOWERS?

Mother's Day falls on the fourth Sunday in Lent in the United Kingdom and on the second Sunday in May in most of the rest of the world, and it is one of the busiest days in the floral calendar. Interestingly enough, the tradition started in Britain when many young people lived "in service" in large houses or estates and were given just one Sunday a year to return home and visit their mothers. In England a tradition was born of taking wild flowers home as a gift, most notably violets plucked from the hedgerows and abundant at that time of year. However, the origins of celebrating mothers actually dates back to ancient Greece: as part of a three-day festival to honour Cybele, the mother of gods, flowers were collected and offered to her.

Another day that is gaining importance for flowers is the International Women's Day, which is held on March 8th every year. It is a major day of global celebration for the economic, political, and social achievements of women. It started out as a political event in Russia and is sometimes also known as Russian Ladies Day. In some celebrations, the day lost its political flavour, and became simply an occasion for men to express their love to the women around them in a way somewhat different than Valentine's and Mother's days. The date is also perfect to celebrate spring!

this page Anemones, *Muscari*, *Viburnum opulus*, 'Blue Diamond' tulips, 'Blue Pacific' roses, 'Weber's Parrot' tulips, 'Atlantic' hyacinths, cream ranunculus, and a touch of birch catkins have been spiraled into a hand-tied bouquet and trimmed with a net and my signature ribbon.

opposite Floral foam wreath rings holding *Pieris japonica*, 'Timeless' roses, camellia, 'Gipsy Queen' hyacinths, *Ranunculus*, and a touch of *Alchemilla mollis* surround green glass candelabra.

right and far right Hand-tied bouquets of massed roses and *Ranunculus* are edged with a frill of camellia leaves. The stems of the flowers are visible through the green plastic pots for added visual interest.

below A 'Timeless' rose trims a napkin with a tie of green beads.

spoil your mother with an elegant lunch

Judging by the huge amount of flowers sold on Mother's Day, it is still a big tradition to give flowers or plants. Most of us take the opportunity to visit our mothers that day if we live close by, spring bouquet or houseplant in hand, or send a floral gift in lieu of a visit if we live too far away or just cannot make it back home. Some years, however, it's nice to invite your mother to your own home, so that you can really spoil her with a special lunch in her honour. To mark the occasion, and to make it just a little bit different from the usual family gathering, why not go to town on the table decorations? You could take as your theme your mother's favorite flower or colors. For most of our designs at this time of year, we use hyacinths with ranunculus and either tulips or anemones. These flowers come in such an excellent choice of colors that you can easily put together a combination that tones nicely.

Here, I've gone for a peach and green theme that feels very ladylike and grown up. Using candelabras on a table always signals a certain formality, but the fact that they are made from green glass prevents them from overpowering the intimate nature of the event. Green glass votive candles are dotted through the design in groups, and I've augmented the floral decorations with strands of green beads for an ultra-feminine touch.

you will need

- 4 6½-inch glass cubes
- 4 4¾-inch glass cubes
- 50 stems of pussy willow
- a pair of scissors
- 30 stems of white 'Carnegie' hyacinths
- 50 stems of 'Weber's Parrot' tulips
- 30 stems of white lilac
- 50 stems of ranunculus
- string

1 Place one of the smaller vases inside one of the larger vases and fill the gap with 5½-inch lengths of pussy willow.

2 Complete each set of 4 vases in the same way, and trim the willow so that it is flush with the top of the vases. Strip all the lower foliage from the stems of the flowers, and then spiral into hand-tied bouquets. Tie with string. Fill the center of the vase with water, and trim the bouquet to fit. Repeat with the three other flowers, using a single type of flower for each bouquet.

3 When the flowers are fitting snugly in the container, cut the tie to loosen up the flower heads so that they cover the tops of the two vases.

Mother's Day quartet

USE A SELECTION OF THE BEST OF THE SPRING FLOWERS
FOR THESE CONTEMPORARY ARRANGEMENTS

birthday bouquets
for someone special

WHY NOT GIVE A LAVISH BOUQUET
BURSTING WITH THE BEST BLOOMS
THAT SPRING CAN OFFER?

When it comes to presenting a gift of flowers to someone on their birthday, it's always nice to send something with a personal touch, rather than a generic bouquet that is already made up for you when you arrive at your local florist. Of course it's always lovely to be given flowers, and only the most ungrateful person would not appreciate the gesture, even if the bouquet was not to their particular taste. But if you put just a little thought into what goes into your bouquet, to make it really special to that person, the recipient will immediately respond to your aesthetic choices as well as the generosity of the gift itself. In other words, they will like it that much more!

Color is always a good starting point, and you can make your selection based around that. Equally, a single favorite flower, such as an individual rose, can be the inspiration for a whole design. Or you can make an extravagant gesture: if you know the person you are buying for really loves pink tulips, buy a large number of them and make them up into one huge hand-tied bouquet.

The seasonal approach is always best: not only will you get much better value for your money and be buying flowers in their very peak condition, but many people make a subconscious link between the time of the year that they were born and what's coming into bloom around that time. It's almost as though we think nature itself is putting on a show in celebration of our birthdays!

left and opposite Color is the theme of this hand-tied bouquet, with orange predominating the selection of ivy berries, brachyglottis, sandersonia, *Papaver*, 'Apricot Parrot' tulips, mimosa, *Myrica gale* myrtle foliage, *Rosa* 'Fiesta+,' and the guelder rose.

this page Perfect for someone with a green thumb: this bouquet of prunus, blue anemones, white ranunculus, hellebores, camellia, ivy berries, lilac, and 'Monte Carlo' tulips is like a miniature spring garden.

this page Men often respond to exotic plants and sculptural shapes. *Phormium tenax* 'Variegatum', *Nelumbo*, *Hypericum* 'Jade Flair', *Tillandsia*, and some white 'Maureen' tulips form a suitably masculine-feeling bouquet.

you will need

- a 12-inch floral foam wreath with plastic tray
- 80 to 100 "Happy" roses
- a knife
- some medium weight stub wires
- a straight-sided 10-inch glass bowl
- floating wax decorations

1 Soak the ring in water until the air bubbles cease to rise. Shave the corners off the outer and inner edges of the wreath frame to give a more rounded outline.

2 Remove the petals from three of the roses, and pin them into the center edge of the ring to cover the foam and tray, using stub wires. Trim the roses to about 2½ inches and remove any foliage. Place a row of four roses running from the outer to the inner edge of the bowl, pushing the stems into the foam. Place the bowl into the center to make sure the inner rose is positioned correctly.

3 Continue around the ring working from the outside to the inside. Remove the bowl again, which will make it easier to work on the wreath. Continue adding all the roses all the way round the ring. When completed add the bowl, fill with water, and add the floating wax decorations.

birthday party bonanza

RAINBOW-DYED ROSES ARE GREAT FOR CHILDREN'S PARTIES
BECAUSE THEY ARE JUST SO COLORFUL

summer

summer
inspirations

THIS IS QUITE SIMPLY THE VERY BEST SEASON FOR FLOWER ARRANGING. THE ABUNDANT
HARVEST THAT SUMMER OFFERS TOPS ANY OTHER SEASON FOR THE FLOWER LOVER

I particularly treasure the beginning of summer when we have just tipped over the edge
of spring and everything is shooting upward and outward. I love the lush English
hedgerows filled with towering Queen Anne's Lace, which gives an *Alice in Wonderland*
feeling to a simple walk. Nature feels on tip-top form, and after a few days of heavy rain
everything in the natural world shoots up like a slightly exaggerated dream. There are a
few very special wild flowers that are out and I adore, such as the ox-eye daisies and the
foxgloves on the banks and under the trees. The mid-summer period where everything
looks like it needs water, and the grass goes to seed, I am less fond of, but at the end
of the season summer redeems itself with the large-headed sunflowers, the showy
dahlias, the huge heads of sedum and hydrangea, and all the trailing amaranthus.

Summer flowers are plentiful, and so this is the time to try more ambitious designs.
The opportunities for outdoor entertaining make this a perfect time to show off your
bouquet and wreath-making skills, and higher levels of light mean you can use more
vivid color schemes and palettes. Summer is also a great time for studying flowers and
learning from nature. From our gardens or parks you can see what combinations work
well, and by looking at how plants grow you can inform your cut flower choices.

At this time of year we can really
enjoy the fact that we can cut
flowers in the garden with complete
abandon, because tomorrow the
summer will provide us with more!
Garden roses mixed with dill,
astrantia, astilbe, feverfew, and
blown peonies are just a few of the
season's beauties that inspire me
at the start of each summer.

During the summer months I often find I am drawn towards using glass in many of my designs, perhaps because of the higher light levels. This glass urn is filled with a bursting bouquet of delphinium, molucella, hydrangea, dahlias, peonies, trailing amaranthus, leycesteria, *Miscanthus* 'Rotfeder,' astilbe, antirrhinum, *Alchemilla mollis*, poppy seed heads, *Pennisetum*, and *Panicum* 'Warrior'.

what summer
means to me

The summer is a good time for slowing down the pace of life and enjoying time with friends. It's a time for casual dining, lots of outdoor entertaining, and fun. I love sitting in my garden and marveling at the height of the perennials that were hidden during the winter. I often find myself wandering through the flowerbed looking for which plants have done well and which have lost out to more aggressive varieties. As a florist, I pick my garden plants because I love the flowers, rather than for their position in the garden, so very often in my summer garden it is a case of survival of the fittest!

Summer means lots of scents. I love the early morning or late evening fragrances of philadelphus, honeysuckle, lavender, and jasmine. It is a time for gathering herbs to make tisanes and salads. I love the color palettes of summer, which evolve in strength as the summer progresses. At the start of the summer season, there are lots of flowers in shades of blue, lilac, and pink; it is a great time to indulge in peonies, delphiniums, lupins, and foxgloves. Although you can always find pink flowers, this is the best time of year for my most favoured color. The choice in pink is truly magnificent, and later in the year when the summer starts to wane all my favorite yellow flowers start to take over: glorious sunflowers, heleniums, *Alchemilla mollis*, and lovely dill and fennel.

The larger-headed flowers of the summer season are best for dramatic vase arrangements or large wreath arrangements. For big bouquets, use delphiniums and blowsy roses with peonies and garden roses. For wreaths, I love to use groups of roses and round-headed flowers. Tall spires of delphiniums and molucella are not a suitable choice for wreaths, as there is too much waste, but small delicate spires of lysimachia give movement to table or door wreaths. Small flowers such as nigella, cornflowers, and pinks look great in tiny bouquets, or can be used in groups in wreaths, and I particularly like to use bundles in wreaths. Lavender works particularly well, either fresh or dried.

a riot of color

THIS IS THE TIME OF YEAR FOR YOU TO TRY REALLY
ADVENTUROUS COLOR COMBINATIONS

this page A cube filled with colored
gravel is topped with a bouquet of
purple phlox, pink *Ozothamnus
diosmifolius*, nepenthes,
Gomphocarpus physocarpus 'Moby
Dick,' *Rosa* 'Vampire' and 'Shadow,'
and striped 'Sunlife' calla lilies.

I am fascinated by the relationship of temperature to color, and how that manifests itself. The summer sun invites us to assemble all the wonderful colors of nature together. It is my belief that you can make any color work with any other—as they do in nature—if you have the right amount of greenery, and if you mix colors in the right amount of intensity. In flower arranging the best way to do this is to use the flowers in groups of colors. Both these arrangements are great examples of this technique.

this page A mossed wreath has been based with ivy berries and red skimmia, and then groups of 'Aqua!' roses, gloriosa lilies, dark 'Colandro' roses, 'Mistique' and 'Serena' gerberas, baby eggplants, limes, and yellow capsicums have been wired into the frame.

you will need

- 10 stems of white delphinium
- 10 stems of white calla lilies
- 10 stems of 'Avalanche+' roses
- 10 stems of white 'Pompei' lilies
- 8 stems of *Viburnum opulus* 'Roseum'
- 8 stems of molucella
- 8 stems of *Syringa* 'Madame Florent Stepman'
- 10 stems of white larkspur
- 8 stems of antirrhinums
- 10 stems of lime green kangaroo paw (*Anigozanthos flavidus*)
- a bunch of trailing smilax (*Asparagus asparagoides*)
- string or floral tie
- a pair of scissors
- a large vase

1 Strip all the lower foliage from the stems so that half of the stem is completely clean and free from any debris. Lay out all your flowers of each variety, and then start by taking the first central flower between your thumb and first finger; add five pieces of plant material at right angles to the first piece, and then twist in your hand. Add another five and twist again, and continue adding and twisting until you have a well-balanced natural bouquet. Tie firmly with string or floral tie. Trim the ends of the stems with a diagonal cut.

2 Fill the vase with water mixed with flower food. Place the bouquet in the center of the vase. Untie the tie to loosen the stems a little. Place one end of the smilax into the water and trail the other end around the edge of the vase to create a natural collar.

summer glory

THIS COMBINATION OF WHITE AND GREEN
IS VIBRANT AND FRESH AND WILL STAND UP TO
THE INTENSE LIGHT LEVELS OF HIGH SUMMER

summer weddings

this page   A tied bouquet of tight 'Margaret Merril' rosebuds bound with silk and a pearl prom corsage bracelet makes a stunning bridal bouquet.

this page A ring of *Paphopedilum* Rosy Dawn heads bound together with florist's wire and trimmed with decorative pearl wire makes a beautifully elegant headdress.

The summer is always a busy time for me, as it is still the most popular season for weddings, so from June to September many weekends are taken up with the joy of arranging wedding flowers. At this time there is an abundance of plant material on offer and it can be quite daunting for brides to make a choice. Whatever color you have chosen for your wedding, I always feel that it is best to make sure the bridal flowers are appropriate and really complement the dress. As most brides still get married in ivory or a shade of white, then wedding bouquets and accessories in these shades still remain the most popular and suitable choice. My favorite seasonal white flowers are peonies, sweet peas, and lily-of-the-valley. The garden roses and orchids shown here are also hard to top! The arrangements on these pages have also been accessorized with different pearl trims. There are a number of products now available specifically for the bridal market, and so if you like a little "bling" with your flowers you can now, with apologies to Shakespeare, literally "gild the lily!"

you will need

- 10 stems of Clooney ranunculus
- a bunch of pink jasmine
- 2 bunches of pink sweet peas
- 2 bunches of purple sweet peas
- 5 'Sarah Bernhardt' peonies
- 8 stems of astrantia
- a selection of different sized florist wires
- a roll of green floral tape
- a pack of lilac skeletonized leaves
- a roll of silver wire
- a length of pink ribbon
- a pearl-headed pin

1 Remove all the flower heads from their stems, and wire using the appropriate sized florists' wire. The larger heads should be wired internally by placing the wire into the stem and up into the flower head. With branches of flowers, like the astrantia ,you can place a thin silver wire through a branch and loop one length of the wire over the other and the stem three times. Delicate stems of jasmine and sweet pea can be wired in the same way. Cover the wire with the green floral tape.

2 Start to place all the flowers into a nice round bouquet shape. Take care not to cross your wires, and use a mirror so you can see the shape you are creating. Be careful with your bouquet, and stand it up in a heavy jug when you need to put it down—to avoid damaging the delicate flowers. Wire the skeletonized leaves with a double-leg mount and place them round the bouquet. Bind in one place with a roll of silver wire.

3 Bind down the stem with a ribbon, slightly diagonally, and then back up the other side and either secure with a pearl-headed pin pushed into the center of the bouquet or by tying on with a bow.

bridal bouquet

SUMMER FLOWERS HAVE THE VERY BEST
SCENTS, AND SWEET PEAS AND JASMINE
ARE AMONG THE MOST EVOCATIVE
FOR WEDDINGS

centerpieces for special occasions

SEASONAL SUMMER BLOOMS REALLY LEND THEMSELVES TO FLORAL SHOWPIECES FOR CELEBRATORY TABLE DECORATIONS

this page Perfect for the top table at a wedding: a low crystal candelabra with a ring of white scabious, snowberry, 'Margaret Merril,' 'Julia's Baby,' and 'Blue Moon' roses, *Ammi visnaga*, and *Symphoricarpos* 'Charming Fantasy.'

opposite, above A Perspex candelabra with a domed wreath of massed Clooney ranunculus is a pretty and modern take on a formal look.

opposite, below A ring at the base of the candelabra has been filled with peonies, dill, grasses, garden roses, and astrantia for a loose natural feel.

candelabras
Although the widespread availability of electricity has phased out our functional need for candles, candlesticks, and candelabras, they are still used as a decorative element or to add atmosphere on special occasions. Currently, there is a enormous popularity for candlelight, and as a consequence an enormous industry has grown up supplying candles in every color, size, and scent and a candlestick or candelabra to suit!

I think one of the reasons candlelight is so precious to so many is because it is has been used throughout history in the religious ceremonies of many different faiths. For Sikhs, candles are used for Diwali, the festival of light. For those of the Buddhist faith it is used along with incense and flowers for ritual observances, and candles are lit in most Hindu homes too. For Christians candles are lit for services or for remembrance, and in Jewish homes candles are lit every Friday night as well as for many of the festivals. For cultural and historical reasons we also turn to candlelight to decorate our wedding tables.

You can use floral foam rings to decorate candelabras either at the base or, if resting on the branches that hold the candles, at the top. Rings around the base are better for lower candelabras where a more intimate feeling is required, whereas rings around the top are better for larger and taller candelabras that are going to be placed in a grand room with high ceilings. The rings come in many different sizes, from 8 inches up to nearly 24 inches, so there is a size to suit any function. For contract work, we also have rings that are plastic backed, which I prefer as they seem to hold more water than the polystyrene-backed rings. If I am using one tightly around a base, I may cut it in one place so that I can get it around the base, but I prefer to use a ring which is large enough to fit around the candelabra without being cut. First soak the ring in tepid water for about five minutes. If you have flower food, add this to the water as it will enhance the life of the ring. When the air bubbles cease to rise, you are ready to begin your flower arrangement and can start by "greening up," or adding the greenery. I prefer to use large leaves around the base, such as galax or bigger varieties of ivy. Work from the base into the center, taking care to hide the underside, so when your guests sit at the table they cannot see the mechanics, only the gorgeous flowers and foliages.

using mirrors Placing a mirror disk in the center of a table is a tried-and-tested way of making your centerpiece stand out. The reflection of the arrangement magnifies the effect of the flower and adds another dimension. It also works well if you use votives or candles, as it reflects this light, making a very sparkly effect. It helps to protect the table from damage from water or candle wax, and also helps to protect heirloom linens. There is a range of sizes you can buy, and my most used is 8½ inches for large banquet tables.

Some hotels provide mirrors in the hire of the hall and in some cases if they do not come as standard you can rent them through your caterer or florist. For a really sparkly party we cut acrylic mirror and decorate the entire table top, which looks very effective. You can also do this with black or tinted mirror. Black shiny acrylic with black tables looks smart. For a recent 50th wedding anniversary we topped the tables with cream flowers in glass containers, and I think the combination of the black and cream looked very chic.

Mirror is a device for making a few flowers look much more special, and I think it worth investing in a few discs or squares for your own home. Round mirrors are also good for protecting your tables from damage from a soaked wreath frame, so they are practical as well as visually attractive! If you have a long table ask a glass cutter to cut you a piece to fit, and use it with votives and some mirror cubes for a very simple but stylish effect. I often line trays with mirror for serving canapés, as that is also visually very attractive.

opposite Limequats sit in a glass wreath vase with five perfect gardenia flowers and white floating candles.

below 'Chianti' calla lilies and tropical *Diplocyclos palmatus* vine swirl around a ring of glass balls. If the flowers are to be reflected from below you must choose only the most perfect specimens.

you will need

- a 12-inch plastic-backed floral foam ring
- 2 bunches of galax
- a pack of thin taper candles
- 2 bunches of *Brachyglottis* 'Sunshine'
- at least 50 stems of sweet peas
- a pair of scissors

1 Soak the ring for five minutes in tepid water. If you have some flower food then place it into the bowl as well as it will help feed the flowers and counteract any bacteria. Before adding any flowers, green up the ring with the foliage. I like to use plastic-backed wreath frames wherever possible, and to edge the ring with large leaves. One of the easiest to use are galax. I find these to be just the right size and also they have lovely tough stems which are easier to insert into the foam.

2 After you have edged all round the ring, add the senecio at different angles, creating a lovely rounded effect.

3 Finally add the sweet peas, working from one end of the ring to the other, taking care to put them in at different heights and depths around the frame. Sweet peas have very delicate stems and so it is vital that you hold your hand as near to the flower heads as possible and push them into the foam very carefully, to avoid breaking their fragile stems. Finally, add the candles by pushing down firmly into the soaked foam.

scented circle

DELICATE MULTICOLORED SWEET PEAS ARE
SET OFF BEAUTIFULLY BY THE TEXTURED
FOLIAGE BACKGROUND

girlie birthdays

I TAKE MY INSPIRATION FROM VIBRANT FABRICS WHEN THINKING OF BIRTHDAY FLOWERS FOR FEMALE FRIENDS

These occasions are the perfect time to indulge in a little over-the-top color and decoration. I often think of overblown floral prints or an accessory that is very feminine, such as jewelry or ribbon. Attaching ribbon to ribbed glasses or vases can produce a very eye-catching color effect. Even the odd well-placed bow can transform an old container. Striped or spotted fabric simply tied around a bowl vase with cord is another quick way of producing a lovely colored vase if you do not fancy floral prints. If you are adapting containers it is always safer to use one flower or a single variety of flower in lots of colors. The easiest choice for this is flowers from the gerbera family, particularly the smaller germini variety and, of course, roses, which you can get in lots of colors whatever the season, although they are still thought of as a summer flower.

above left Mixed blowsy Equadorian roses are arranged simply as a hand-tied bouquet then placed in a smart black glass cube vase to highlight the fabulous variety of colors.

below left Ultra feminine and ultra pretty: a domed hand-tied bouquet of 'Rosita Vendela' roses sits in a plastic pot that has been spray-painted shocking pink to match.

opposite, center Glass jewels have been placed into a fluted vase and a dome of germini gerberas placed on top. A wreath of hot-glued jewels has been placed at the base.

this page The dark dahlias and the black centers on the germini gerberas make these vibrant late summer bunches coordinate perfectly. All the flowers chosen have vibrant colors as well as lovely textures. The lime green flowers are large marigolds—mixed here with dill they help to make the colors of the gerberas, dahlias, and stocks really vibrant.

all wrapped up

I personally like to use natural wrappings, such as by-products of the coconut family. Large leaves also make a great trim, so we often fold aspidistra leaves around a bunch to protect the flower heads. Banana leaves also make great wrapping, especially if you buy the lengths that have been cut from each side of the spine of a larger leaf. These are packaged in Thailand, boxed, and flown all over the world for use in Asian cookery or for catering display. We purchase these especially from the fruit and vegetable wholesale market that adjoins the flower market in London.

left Peonies, phlox, sweet peas, *Alchemilla mollis*, hebe, and rosemary are surrounded by a collar formed from cut sections of banana leaves.

opposite, top left Trails of jasmine and a decadent pink feather trim that echoes the airy feel of the astilbe and *Alchemilla mollis* augment a grouped bouquet of 'Barbie' roses, campanula, and hydrangea flowers.

opposite, top right I love the feel and colors of the fabric wraps made in Korea or China. Two-toned 'Fiesta+', pink and brown 'Two Faces+,' and cream 'Lemonade' roses, Oriental poppies, cestrum, *Ozothamnus diosmifolius* 'Champion Pink,' and green kangaroo paw (*Anigozanthos*) are aqua packed and wrapped with soft peach fabric.

opposite, below left Mixed dahlias have been generously swathed with matching pink fabric wrap.

opposite, below right Roses, campanula, astrantia, and sestrum have been swaddled in lilac wrap and placed in a special bouquet bag.

Swathe your bouquet in something special to transform it into a gift

Over the twenty years that I have been working as a professional florist we have used a number of different types of wrapping. My favorites are hand made Thai paper from kozo or mulberry pulp or, when the budget allows, a very special handmade Japanese paper with added petals or flower heads.

take one bouquet...

I have always loved these little tea glasses, and I often use them for individual miniature bouquets that I either dot randomly around the table or position next to each place setting. Taking my cue from the elegant purple and gilt decoration, I chose a selection of beautiful high summer blooms in the blue and mauve spectrum, including sweet peas, scabious, veronica, and roses, with red-tinged astrantia and thistles as an accent color. The feeling is loose and airy—the suggestion is of a bouquet that could easily have been gathered from the garden on a summer's evening.

Taking the idea a step further to form a centerpiece, I gathered a number of the filled glasses in a circle on a purple plate, securing them with floral tac. I then infilled with extra flowers and foliage between each glass and on the inner and outer sides to complete the wreath shape.

this page The secret with working with small containers such as this one is to keep the stem length of all the flowers short, so the overall shape remains compact. This is especially true when you are working with a combination of different flower shapes and sizes.

opposite From the top the wreath forms a tight circle, and its shape can be appreciated; the glasses also give it a certain amount of height. The soft fluffy green flower heads of *Lagurus* grass, with their sword-like leaves poking through, form a counterpoint to the densely massed flowers.

...and make a wreath

take one bouquet...

In my vase and bowl collection I have lots of different vessels that are not very deep and tend to suit small flowers. There are many ways of using them and although it is tempting to use floral foam, delicate summer flowers prefer to be in water, so I often make a number of small bouquets. Often I use grids of Scotch Tape or florist tape to make the bowls more serviceable for flowers, and to help keep the small bouquets upright. I find this large grouping of small flowers very effective. It can also can serve as a going away "thank you" present for your guests. This is a lovely touch and always very much appreciated.

...and make a trough

The trick to making really tight and neat small bouquets is to be very careful to remove all the lower foliage and flower heads from the stem. You are going to need to hold your hand very near to the top of the stem to make the spiral and so clean stems are imperative. You can save some of the longer branches for use around the edge of the bouquets. Try to pick flowers with similar size heads and certainly none that are any larger than 1½ inches. I find this kind of arrangement is best in summer when there are lots of small flowers to choose from, and you can use several different varieties. I love sweet peas, lysimachia, veronica, flowering mint, feverfew, and spray of roses for the bouquets.

below A low silver and glass trough has been filled with four individual posies of dill, scabious, echinops, cornflower, ivy berries, and that indispensable summer filler plant, *Alchemilla mollis*.

party decorations

FLOWERS CELEBRATE WITH US ON OUR BIRTHDAYS, AT
ANNIVERSARIES, AND AT FAMILY PARTIES, AND SUMMER
IS THE BEST TIME TO CREATE YOUR OWN DECORATIONS

It is a great pleasure to work with flowers and so lovely to be able to make
bouquets and wreaths to celebrate memorable occasions. The most successful
celebration flowers are those that suit the occasion and the host, and are in
season. I have arranged lots of parties over the years with seasonal flowers, and
some with flowers that were not, and the most effective were those when
seasonal flowers were used to their best advantage. They are the best value and
when used at their peak they speak for themselves, however you design them!

For celebrations, you need the flowers to be at their best, which means that
you need to buy them and condition them for your event. The timings on this
will depend on the temperature of your home and the time of year. It will also
depend on which varieties you select. Some flowers, such as lilies, take a week
to open, especially more sophisticated hybrids, whereas others such as sweet
peas and delphiniums are very short lived and best used fresh. Most flowers are
somewhere in between and need a couple of days to look best, such as roses,
peonies, and summer border blooms such as achillea, larkspur, dahlias, and the
like. Learning when to buy flowers and how to look after them can be trial and
error, but you will soon get to know how to get the party flower look together!

this page Orange and pink celosia as well as orange asclepias are used with contrasting groups of peach, orange, and pink roses around a storm lantern. Little vases of gloriosa encircle the arrangement.

opposite Dahlias with wired kumquats make a very textural effect for the wreath, around a kumquat-filled vase of dahlias.

you will need

- a 14-inch plastic-backed floral foam ring
- a floristry knife
- a selection of foliage—I used hebe, pistachio berries, *Alchemilla mollis*, and galax leaves
- 15 roses
- 15 peony tulips
- 3 bunches of white sweet peas
- 10 stems of white phlox
- 5 stems of eustoma

1 Trim the edge of the foam ring after soaking it in water for ten minutes. Then place the larger leaves around the edge and mix the foliage so that it is at different heights and lengths around the ring.

2 When the foliage is all the way around the ring, you can begin to add the flowers. First place the roses at different heights and depths around the ring and then begin to add the more fragile flowers such as the sweet peas.

3 Continue adding the flowers, taking care with the peony tulips to hold your hand close to the foam so that you can gently ease the stem into the ring. Keep the foam very damp as these delicate summer flowers will need lots of water.

ring of cheer

HUNG ON YOUR FRONT DOOR,
THIS GLORIOUS SUMMER
WREATH WOULD BE A
FANTASTIC WELCOME
FOR YOUR GUESTS

opposite Grouping allows you to put together flowers that may not be in harmony in another style of arrangement. Green hydrangea, poppy seedheads, and grasses have been grouped in a ring around a glass candle bowl with summer flowers such as agapanthus, blue bee, larkspur, stocks, eryngium, triteleia, and groups of blue viburnum berries.

right If you find you have a lot of one particular flower, a single-variety wreath is an effective way of making good use of them. This simple arrangement is made from the heads of 'Supernova' Questar eryngium pushed into a floral foam ring.

While generally it is hard to grow enough to pick for a large celebration, there is always something in my garden I can use to supplement some bought flowers. When choosing flowers for your garden, it is always good to think about planting varieties with different habitats, to give you some tall line flowers, some dominant flowers, and some filler flowers, in addition to foliage. Flowers that I grow for length are delphiniums, flag irises, and lupins. I also like to have some agapanthus, alliums, and nerines because they have a lovely architectural quality to them. My focal flowers are usually roses, peonies, lilies, dahlias, and sunflowers. My favorite fillers are *Alchemilla mollis*, grasses, echinops, eryngium, and seedheads such as rudbeckia and poppies.

Unless I have a glut of flowers, I usually plan my garden flower arrangements as either loose bouquets of a mixture of flowers or, if I am making a wreath, a grouped ring. The blue flowers (left) show how you can use different varieties in groups that would be very hard to use in a massed or mixed design. Heavy groups of greenery also help to tone shapes and colors together.

If I am lucky enough to have a glut of one type of flower, then the most effective way of making a great display is by using them en masse as we have with the eryngium ring (above). Some of the most effective parties I have ever designed have used only one type of flower. Favorites have included hydrangea, peonies, roses, and even the humble carnation!

you will need

- 2 glass containers, one small enough to fit inside the other
- a selection of small green apples
- a bunch of white scabious
- a bunch of poppy seedheads
- 2 branches of ivy berries
- some garden roses
- a bunch of *Alchemilla mollis*
- 5 heads of white hydrangea
- a bunch of *Ammi visnaga*
- a pair of scissors
- some wire for tying

1 Place one container inside the other one and fill the gap with small green apples. Fill the central container with water mixed with flower food.

2 Clean the lower stems so that they are free from foliage and thorns and spiral into a hand-tied bouquet. Trim the flowers so that they are quite short and easy to handle.

3 Tie with the wire and then diagonally cut each stem so that it is exactly the right height to sit at the top of the vase. Place it in the vase and top up with water.

fruits and flowers

THE SUMMER ABUNDANCE EXTENDS
TO THE ORCHARDS AS WELL AS THE
FLOWER BEDS, AND USING SMALL
FRUITS IS A GREAT WAY TO ADD
INTEREST TO GLASS CONTAINERS

the fall

fall
inspirations

AS THE TEMPERATURES DROP AND THE DAYS GROW SHORTER, THE STUNNING SHAPES AND COLORS OF THE FALLEN LEAVES ARE A GREAT INSPIRATION, AS ARE THE BARREN OUTLINES OF THE NAKED TREES

Fall has always been a favorite time of year for me. The melancholy feeling that starts to descend as the summer sun fades feels a more appropriate time of year for "turning over a new leaf" than the beginning of a new calendar year. I think that this feeling is in part the legacy of childhood years spent at school, and then my early working career as a teacher, where the end of summer marks a new beginning with a different class. But also it is the finale of the growing season, and for the gardener it is the end of the hopes for this year's garden and the start of the planning for next year.

I find myself very drawn to bulb catalogues as I start to plan and look forward to the next cycle of growth. For the floral decorator, the start of the colder seasons means that there is now more focus on the interior of the house and the heavy decorating months are upon us. The other reason the fall means so much to me is that it is an interesting time of year because the low light levels and the changes in the landscape make your choice of flowers and foliages more vibrant. Just as we naturally turn to heavier foods during the cooler months, our taste for heavier decorations and more pronounced color schemes also follows. My designs naturally become more textural as we use fruits, vegetables, nuts, and seedheads with flowers and foliages.

It's not so much about the flowers for this season, but the trees and the bushes and all the seedheads and berries they bear. Oak, larch, laurel, cotoneaster, hydrangea, crab apples, apples, walnuts, dried oranges, and solaniums are just some of the bounty around at this time of year.

This wonderfully textural wreath, set on a base of a mossed ring, has an abundant fall mix of *Viburnum opulus* berries, apples, chestnuts, some very realistic fake mushrooms, lotus seedheads, alder catkins, and berries from the *Solanum integrifolium* climber.

what the fall
means to me

The fall is an interesting mixture of emotions: on the one hand the landscape is screaming out in full technicolor, but because of the lower light levels and declining temperatures we tend to spend more time inside. First the fruits of the forest give us inspiration, and sweet and horse chestnuts and little acorns are personal favorites of mine. I still cannot take a walk in the fall without picking up treasures to bring home. The squishy red berries of *Viburnum opulus* are first to herald the start of the fall, closely followed by cotoneaster, ivy, and ligustrum, and by the time we start to see the stunning purple berries of the *Callicarpa* bushes, the fall is on the wane and winter is setting in.

The newly undressed trees and bushes at this time of year are perfect for bouquets and wreaths. Apart from contorted willow and hazel, I am huge fan of the genus *Cornus* with its numerous species. The vivid red stems of *Cornus alba* 'Elegantissima' are great for placing on the inside of vases or working into large hand-tied bouquets. In the garden I love to see the stunning yellow fall stems of *Cornus sericea* 'Flaviramea.' The other great treasures of the the fall are the male catkins of the hazel and the alder, which give a lovely flow to arrangements. The alders have the lovely elongated male catkins in the fall with the smaller mature female catkins still intact, which resemble small cones and often get confused with mulberries because they are similar in shape. I adore these relaxed and bendy branches woven into lovely wreaths.

fabulous foliage

THE FALL IS THE BEST TIME FOR MAKING FOLIAGE-HEAVY BOUQUETS AND WREATHS BECAUSE THERE IS SUCH A PLETHORA OF MATERIAL AVAILABLE

From the kitchen garden I love to use kales that have gone to seed by removing the lower leaves, and of course there are now many ornamental kales sold through the Dutch flower auctions. Once they were an autumnal treat, but now they are popular because they are long lasting and presumably easy to cultivate, which makes them quite inexpensive. The brassicas have a great texture and a good chunky rosette, which makes them both a good filler or a focal "flower"—not bad for a smelly vegetable!

this page Groups of viburnum berries, variegated *Viburnum tinus*, hypericum, camellia, kales, and a little eucalyptus for scent, are enclosed in a collar of glossy curled aspidistra leaves.

this page This cheerful fall mix includes roses, hips, flowering eucalyptus, larch, orange dill, kales, and some spiky standard chrysanthemums.

using fruit, nuts, and berries

BLACKBERRIES, DAMSONS, CRAB APPLES, AND OTHER SMALL FRUITS ALWAYS ADD TEXTURE AND COLOR TO ARRANGEMENTS

At this time of year, I also love to use chestnuts in vases topped with bouquets or make a collection of fall "finds," and then dress the table with leaves, vines, and nuts with lots of candles and votives. If you have a glut of apples, they look great as votive holders. Find some lovely colored apples with flat bottoms and then cut a small hole at the top to fit a metal tea light into snugly. In the the fall I can always find a few dahlia heads, and these look good floating in a large bowl with some candles. Also, try using lots of berries in a bowl with floating candles, as that looks very effective too. Autumnal leaves make great containers when wrapped around old jars for small fall bouquets or single heads of standard chrysanthemums.

I am growing callicarpa berries in my own garden as I adore their iridescent purple color, which looks great floating in bowls or as sprigs in tiny fall bouquets. Callicarpa also looks very effective in purple wreaths or tied to miniature bouquets on a napkin.

I adore ligustrum berries and hips, and I mix them with other foliage such as members of the viburnum family and the eucalyptus family, which add their own fragrance. There are also still a lot of herbs to be found in the fall: sage, rosemary, and some woody lavender can all be combined with nuts and berries to add a layer of scent.

left This rectangular-framed wreath was made from lengths of alder bound together with reel wire and tied in the corners with string. It is decorated with branches of catkin-bearing larch and dried okra, whole and sliced limes, apple slices, and lichen moss.

opposite A very natural-feeling and loose hanging wreath uses a range of autumnal greenery including *Garrya elliptica*, cotoneaster, ivy berries, larch, and lichen, with red berries and red skimmia for fall glory.

left I decorated this twig ring with the fruits and seedheads of the *Physalis* plant, known as Chinese lanterns. These were glued in place and rosehips were then wired in place around them.

rings for the fall

This is the time of year to dust off your hot glue gun and invest in a pair of heat-proof gloves, and then you will be ready to create beautiful seasonal and long-lasting rings. In the the fall you can find lots of these seedheads, dried fruits, and spices being offered at flower markets, but you can also try dried flower companies if you want to create a more permanent decoration for your home. You can make a natural ring from vines, branches, dried mosses, or even straw, or you can use a floral foam ring as a base. Large items, whose weight is considerable, will need to be wired onto a wreath as the glue will not hold them for very long when the wreath is suspended.

I am particularly fond of using crab apples and cranberries in my decorations in the fall months, either pinned into wreaths or concealing the stems of bouquets in clear glass vases. Glossy chestnuts make great wreaths if you use a glue gun to stick them onto a moss frame. Mixed nuts also look great because you get the varied texture from the different shapes and patterns on the shells. In the Netherlands lots of small-sized apples, pears, and even artichokes are sold in trays at the flower auctions and these look great wired onto wreaths.

opposite, top left If you are planning to glue a lot of small items such as this star anise you might want to invest in a glue pan. This allows you to use a brush to paint on the hot glue and then you can stick the dried items faster to the dry foam base.

opposite, top right Wired cones have been placed into a moss wreath. Longer cones lie flatter, giving more sense of movement around the ring.

opposite, below right Dried mushrooms have been massed onto a dried foam background and secured in place with hot glue. For extra longevity you could varnish the finished wreath.

opposite, below left For the bark and crab apple wreath, lengths of silver birch bark have been glued to a large floral foam wreath. The crab apples have been wired into the foam. Fruits are all best wired, as they are heavy and fleshy. They are kept in place by the moss tucked in as infill.

Seek out unusual materials to make striking and durable decorations

The wreaths shown on this page were bought from our foliage suppliers but you can make similar ones yourself. The techniques are time-consuming, but these rings last a long time—indefinitely if you use all dried materials—so your efforts will be rewarded over many seasons to come.

you will need

- a bag of sphagnum moss
- a 14-inch wire frame
- a reel of heavy wire
- a pair of scissors
- a mixture of fresh fruit: apples, clementines, limes, and lemons
- a mixture of dried fruit: limes, orange slices, and apple slices
- a selection of heavy stub wires
- a bag of mixed whole nuts
- a hot-glue gun

1 Tease out the moss to remove any foreign bodies such as leaves or cones. Attach the reel wire to the inside of the wire frame and then bind handfuls of moss onto the frame.

2 Continue all the way around the ring until you have a firm ring of sphagnum moss. Trim with the scissors to cut off any straggly ends and then mist to keep damp.

3 Wire up all the dried and fresh fruits. Most can be wired by placing a wire through the fruit and placing one leg of the wire over the other three times. The floristry term for this is a *double leg mount*. Wiring is time consuming, and this heavily decorated wreath will take several hours to prepare.

4 Add the bulk of the fresh fruit in groups and then add the dried fruits in the gaps to try to cover as much of the sphagnum moss as possible. It is best to try to place the wires in to the moss in one direction and then bend the wire back the other way, so you create a loop in the moss rather than leaving it straight. Finally, use a hot-glue gun to secure the nuts among the fruits.

fruited ring

YOU DON'T HAVE TO RELY ON FLOWERS
FOR GLORIOUS COLOR AND
TEXTURE

harvest home

opposite A white twig ring has been decorated naturally using clumps of moss, ivy berries, waxed apples, parsnips, baby ears of corn, and three ornamental kales.

right Fiery fall leaves are the color inspiration for this hand-tied bouquet of hips, skimmia, carthamus, beech leaves, and roses, which has been placed into a vase within a fish bowl lined with hot chilli peppers.

Harvest is from the Anglo-Saxon word *haerfest*, which literally translates as "autumn." It later came to refer to the season for reaping and gathering grain and other grown products and foodstuffs. The full moon nearest the autumnal equinox is called the harvest moon. So in ancient traditions harvest festivals were held on or near the Sunday of the harvest moon. Traditionally, this moon is the full moon that falls in the month of September, and thanks have been given for successful harvests since pagan times.

The modern tradition of celebrating harvest festivals in churches began in Britain in 1843, when a Cornish vicar invited his parishioners to sing such Victorian hymns as "We Plough the Fields and Scatter," "Come, Ye Thankful People, Come," and "All Things Bright and Beautiful." This soon became highly popular and the idea of harvest festivals spread, and it became an annual custom. Nowadays, the festival is held at the end of harvest, which varies in different parts of the world. Sometimes neighboring churches will set the harvest festival on different Sundays, so that people can attend each other's celebrations of thanksgiving. The date may change, but the tradition remains the same, and the activities on this day usually include singing hymns, praying, and decorating churches with baskets of home-grown produce, food from the backyard or the farmer's fields to distribute among the less well-off or elderly members of the local community, or to be used to raise funds for the church or a local charity. This now also extends to schools where the "harvest" has moved away from natural produce to more packaged and long-lasting gifts.

The inspiration for any decorations are for whatever is plentiful at that time, and so very often dried seedheads from the harvest may be used, such as wheat, oats, and barley. In my own local church, the flower arrangers look to their backyards and use lots of evergreens with fruits, most notably apples.

you will need

- a bag of sphagnum moss
- a 14-inch wire frame
- a roll of reel wire
- a pair of scissors
- a selection of fresh fruit such as figs, small pears, berries, and crab apples
- dried pomegranates
- 'Scotch Bonnet' peppers
- dried corn cobs
- a bundle of heavy stub wires
- a length of *Diplocyclos palmatus* vine
- a storm lantern
- a pillar candle

1 Tease out the moss to remove any foreign bodies such as leaves or cones. Attach the reel wire to the inside of the wire frame and then bind handfuls of moss onto the frame.

2 Continue all the way around the ring until you have a firm ring of sphagnum moss. Trim with the scissors to cut off any straggly ends and then mist to keep damp.

3 Wire up all the material. Most can be wired by placing a wire through the middle and placing one leg of the wire over the other three times. The floristry term for this is a *double leg mount*. Wiring is time consuming, and this heavily decorated wreath will take several hours to prepare.

4 Place the fruits round the ring in groups, working from the edge into the center. Finally, place the vine through the wreath, and place a storm lantern with a candle into the center.

harvest centerpiece

THIS CHARMING STORM LANTERN RING WOULD
ADD A WELCOMING NOTE TO A HARVEST SUPPER

festivals in the fall

CHILDREN CAN ENJOY THE FUN OF TRICK OR TREAT, WHILE FOR ADULTS
THERE IS THE CHANCE FOR MORE SOPHISTICATED DECORATION

left Black is one of the colors
associated with Halloween. This
grouped ring of black Sumatra twig
includes black lotus seedheads, *Garrya
elliptica*, purple statice, 'Black 'Baccara'
roses, and red hibiscus surrounding
five black candles.

opposite A Halloween hand-tied
bouquet of black-sprayed eryngium,
orange dyed anemones, orange *Ilex*
berries, rosehips, *Hypericum* 'Dolly
Parton,' photinia, black calla lilies,
rudbeckia, chrysanthemums and
contorted willow is edged with spider
fern and wrapped with black fabric.

Halloween

The origin of today's spooky Halloween celebration is in a fusion of many different Christian and pagan festivals. Halloween is on the eve of the religious festival "All Hallows' Day," which according to Catholic theology remembers all those who have become saints and made it to heaven, while the next day, All Souls' Day, commemorates the "departed faithful" who have not yet been purified and reached heaven. The Celts celebrated their new year's eve on October 31st, which fits with my own personal feeling that the fall makes for a far better natural start to the year than January, when we are in the very depths of the winter. It was celebrated every year with a festival called Samhain, that marked the end of the "season of the sun" and the beginning of "the season of darkness and cold," with the beginning of the Celtic new year falling on November 1st.

The Celts believed that evil spirits came with the long hours of winter darkness. They believed on that night the barriers between our world and the spirit world were at their weakest, and therefore spirits were most likely to be seen on earth. There are many different local traditions, which varied in their outcome from predicting witches or even successful marriages. Halloween in England was sometimes called Snap Apple Night. This involved playing a game where apples were suspended on a long piece of string. Contestants had to try to bite the apple without using their hands. This game and a similar one, calling bobbing for apples, where players are asked to try biting an apple suspended in water while wearing a blindfold, are still traditional Halloween party games for children in Britain. The themes of these games carry over into the decorations, with fruits, particularly apples, and nuts being the traditional materials for the flower arranger and great for making into wreaths.

Irish and Scottish immigrants carried versions of the traditional Halloween activities to North America, and although we think of North America as exporting "trick or treating" to the world, that tradition may have come from a ninth-century European custom. During this Christian festival people would make house calls begging for soul cakes. It was believed that even strangers could speed a soul's journey to heaven by saying prayers, so in exchange for a cake they promised to pray for the donors' deceased relatives. Other western countries embraced the holiday and Halloween is now celebrated in several parts of the Western world. As the world becomes more homogeneous, and we are all subject to the same forms of commercial

this page Little buckets decorated with
licorice candies have been filled with
matching bouquets of pink carnations
and roses, kales, lemon gerbera Germinis,
red daisy chrysanthemums, blue
eryngium, and eucalyptus.

marketing, the tradition grows and grows. However, I personally feel that our thoughts on having a little fun in the short and cold days of winter are probably not too dissimilar from our pagan ancestors'!

In terms of floral decoration, Halloween has two very pronounced colors. The first, orange, comes from the jack-o'-lanterns that are carved around the world to welcome strangers to our homes, and the second, black, comes from all things that scare us. Large *Cucurbita* pumpkins can be used as vases by excavating a large hole and placing a plastic container into the hole filled with water mixed with flower food. The smaller *Cucurbita*, of which there is a great variety in colors and shapes, are fantastic wired into wreaths. You can pierce their skins and use a heavy wire.

The huge auctions in the Netherlands produce a number of black items at this time of year. Some are completely natural, such as blackberries, viburnum berries, ligustrum, the black dogwood *Cornus alba* 'Kesselringii,' the darkest calla lily *Zantedeschia* 'Schwarzwalder,' and possibly my two favorites—the dark seedheads of the agapanthus flowers and the giant black capsicums with their rich glossy skins. Increasingly, too, there are lots of dyed items, such as eryngium, *Gomphocarpus frutcosus* 'Moby Dick,' and American oak as well as other foliages. I often mix these with lilac kales and chilli peppers and bright orange flowers such as roses, chrysanthemums, and the season's quintessential Halloween flower, the Chinese lantern *Physalis alkekengi*.

bonfire night

Many places in England combined Halloween with Mischief Night (celebrated on November 4th), when boys played all kinds of practical jokes on their neighbors. They changed shop signs, took gates off their hinges, whitewashed doors, and tied door latches. Certainly in England we later came to celebrate "Bonfire Night" on November 5th after a failed attempt by Catholics to overthrow King James I by blowing up the Houses of Parliament. A mercenary called Guy Fawkes was found in the basement of the Houses of Parliament with 36 barrels of gunpowder and was tortured and executed. To this day we still commemorate this event with huge fireworks displays to commemorate the would-be explosion and bonfires usually burning an effigy of Guy himself.

As time has gone on some of the British have been known, in a tongue-in-cheek kind of way, to question whether they are celebrating the defeat of the Papist plot or honoring the attempt to do away with the government! People in one English town in particular, Lewes in East Sussex, take this tradition very seriously, dressing up in fancy dress and holding several bonfires, with some groups nominating their most "annoying" people of the year to burn as effigies. The multiple colors found in the explosive gunpowder or the tones associated with vibrant fires are usually the chosen palette for these celebrations. Spiky seasonal gladioli, bright gerberas, standard chrysanthemum blooms, and berries are my favorites for creating tall bouquets for this event.

you will need

- 5 'Green Shamrock' chrysanthemums
- 5 sunflowers
- 10 stems of dill
- 10 stems of echinacea
- a few branches of red American oak
- a few branches of red eucalyptus
- a bunch of red skimmia
- 10 stems of green dill
- 5 stems of 'Mango' calla lilies
- some wire-edged tape
- a pair of scissors
- 6½ feet of red fabric wrap
- 5 feet of coordinating ribbon

1 After you have cleaned all the stems of the flowers and foliage and spiraled them neatly into a bunch, tie tightly at the binding point with wire-edged tape. Trim the bottom of the stems so the bouquet stands alone.

2 Cut your fabric wrap in half and then repeatedly fold the fabric so that it is rounded and ruched as shown. Do the same with the other length of wrap and secure it under a heavy object.

3 Place one length half way around the bouquet and the other length around the other half of the bouquet, and then tie them onto the bouquet with a length of ribbon at the same point as the binding point.

4 Make some loops with the length of ribbon; then pinch in the center and tie through the middle with the length of ribbon that you have used to tie the wrap with.

trick or treat

THIS FIERY BOUQUET WOULD
MAKE A GREAT GIFT FOR A
HALLOWEEN PARTY HOSTESS

Thanksgiving

THE COLOR PALETTE IS HOT AND THE EMPHASIS IS ON
DRAMATIC EFFECT IN THESE SEASONAL SHOWSTOPPERS

this page If you are looking for a focal
point for a Thanksgiving dinner, this
amazingly sculptural bouquet would be
it. A hand-tied bunch of skimmia,
chilies, hips, and orange-dyed *Grevillea
longifolia* is supported in a vase filled
with autumnal crab apples and
encircled by contorted willow.

The early settlers took the idea of harvest thanksgiving to North America. On December 4th, 1619, a group of 38 English settlers arrived at Berkeley, about 20 miles upstream from Jamestown. The group made a charter, which required that the day of arrival be commemorated yearly as a "day of thanksgiving" to God. From then on this day became a national celebration in the calendars of both the United States and Canada. This festival is now set on a certain day and has become a national holiday known as Thanksgiving. In North America it has become a national secular holiday with religious origins and is always a Thursday, but it has now become part of a four- or five-day long weekend, which usually marks a pause in school and college calendars. Most employees are given both Thanksgiving and the day after as paid holidays, so this has become a time for reuniting families. As is evidenced by the tremendous level of travel at this time of year, significant effort is made by all family members to gather for the Thanksgiving feast of turkey and all the trimmings.

This is an important time to deck out your home in a welcoming manner, and most front doors across the United States and Canada will sport a door ring to welcome home family. I like to use small fruits and berries for Thanksgiving, and often use a twig base for my door wreath. By late November most of the trees are bare and the sap has started descending, making this a great time to use branches to make wreaths, as the branches are still very pliable. It is also a great time to prune back the yard, and if you cut back vines they also make a perfect backdrop for decorations to create door wreaths. I use some varieties of honeysuckle or *Clematis montana* as they are so vigorous and can be quite invasive in the garden. For table decorations, I often turn at this time of year to the capsicums. We use lots of chili

peppers because it is at this time of year that they become plentiful, and we receive lovely plump bunches of peppers cut on the stem from the Italian growers around San Remo. These look great with other berries and other seasonal flowers and foliages. Another personal favorite for Thanksgiving table decorations is to use bunches of cranberries displayed in the water in glass vases and bowls. These are harvested in water and so last a long time without decaying and make a vase look most attractive.

above A tropical bouquet of grouped snake grass, cymbidium orchids, leucospermum, *Euphorbia fulgens*, aspidistra leaves, swirls of *Liriope gigantea*, and contorted willow is tied with textured paper and orange raffia.

you will need

- a 12-inch foam ring
- a plastic ring tray
- double-sided sticky tape
- a pack of green pipe cleaners
- around 200 small red crab apples
- around 200 pearlized green bead-headed pins

1 Place the foam ring in its plastic tray—there is no need to soak it as you will not be inserting plant material directly into it. Attach a length of the double-sided tape all around the outer edge of the tray, and then firmly stick lengths of the wired pipe cleaners to the tape. Build up neat rows until the tray itself is completely hidden.

2 Remove the stems from the individual crab apples and then pierce each one with a pin, making sure that the pin goes through the top of the apple, at the point where you have removed the stem.

3 Firmly push each apple into the foam, attaching it with the point of the pin. Place the apples tightly together so that no foam shows through, and position the apples at slightly differing heights to create a mounded shape to the wreath. Remember to fill in the inner and outer sides down to the level of the pipe cleaners.

jeweled apples

SOME OF THE MOST EFFECTIVE WREATHS FEATURE
JUST ONE ELEMENT—IN THIS CASE, TINY APPLES

ideas for fall entertaining

The fall is one of the best seasons for napkins ties and place settings as there are so many natural inexpensive items to use. There are abundant vines both from the garden and the wild. I love to prune back my honeysuckle or clematis to make a natural tie for a rolled napkin. Very often I will also add simple place names to the tie, perhaps using parcel labels for a utilitarian look. One of my all-time favorite hedgerow finds are the gray fluffy heads of old man's beard, the wild clematis that grows prolifically in the countryside. The harvest of nuts, cones, and small fruits makes the perfect attachments to a napkin tie, as the scale is ideal. Small pears, either gilded with a fine spray of glitter paint or used naturally, look beautiful positioned next to a place setting carrying a name card. I like also to use a bunch of autumnal leaves with a simple raffia tie for an the fall supper. For more formal parties, I may use a small bouquet constructed of edible plant materials, such a chili peppers, bay leaves, and late-flowering herbs.

opposite, top left A black calla lily and 'Black Baccara' rose with black-dyed eryngium tied to a black pearlized elasticated wrist corsage holder creates a suitably sinister look, with just a hint of black magic!

opposite, top right What could be simpler and yet more elegant? Two cymbidium orchid heads are wired together and attached to bear grass.

opposite, below left Herbs, such as these intertwined stems of thyme and rosemary, make perfect culinary rings.

opposite, below right Miniature bunches of lavender have been wired together to form a scented binding for a napkin.

Unusual and eye-catching table decorations take just a little ingenuity

The range of plant material that is available during the fall months is so varied that you can make mini-wreaths to swathe napkins that will suit any style of occasion, from a casual lunch with a country feel to an elegant dinner party, to create looks from the homespun to the downright glamorous.

you will need

- 10 branches of long contorted willow
- 10 peach gerberas
- 7 stems of *Viburnum opulus*
- 10 stems of *Leucospermum*
- 10 stems of rosehips
- 10 stems of *Asclepias incarnata* 'Cinderella'
- 10 stems of 'Marrakesh' roses
- strong string
- a pair of scissors
- a tall stemmed cocktail glass-shaped vase

1 Fill the container with contorted willow so that it makes a snug nest for the hand-tied bouquet. In spring when the sap is rising and in fall when the sap is declining, willow is still very flexible and can be bent easily without breaking. All the willows are very pliable, which is why they are used in basketry.

2 Remove the foliage from the lower stems and spiral the flowers into a hand-tied bouquet. Tie off the bouquet and trim the bottom off the stems. Weave some willow over the top of the bouquet. Fill the glass with water mixed with flower food and place the bouquet into the nest of contorted willow.

floral cocktail

YOUR GUESTS WILL NOT FAIL TO
BE IMPRESSED BY THIS ELEGANT
TABLE CENTERPIECE

winter

winter
inspirations

THE FRUGALITY OF NATURE DURING THIS SEASON AND THE SCARCITY OF PLANT MATERIAL ARE
CONTRASTED WIDELY WITH THE AMBITIONS AND DESIRES OF FLOWER LOVERS, WHO OFTEN CHOOSE
WINTER TO MAKE THEIR MOST AMBITIOUS AND SHOWY DESIGNS TO CELEBRATE WINTER FESTIVALS

For the winter season, when the textural qualities of nature become much more of
a focus, I find myself being more inspired by the basic shape of trees and bushes
and thinking more deeply about the elements of good design in nature. Winter's
generous abundance of berries is a great stimulation to my creative desires, and
growers and hybridizers have been working hard over recent years to produce more
and more berries to meet increased demands from designers and consumers alike.

My favorite flower of the winter is the humble but arresting steely hellebore.
These shy, nodding-headed flowers bloom from November though April, and there
are three main cultivars used in the cut-flower trade. In the eighteenth century
Helleborus niger was given the common name of the Christmas rose, because the
bowl-shaped cut flowers reminded people of the wild dog roses of the summer.
Helleborus x *hybridus*, which traditionally flower a little later, are known as the
Lenten rose because they are so abundant during the Christian period of Lent. The
other useful variety is *Helleborus argutifolius*, or the Corsican hellebore. The sight
of these beauties pushing up through the frosty earth during the winter months as
a herald of treats to come cannot fail to inspire!

The winter season means hard work
and long hours as we set about the
task of creating long-lasting decorations
from the winter harvest. The traditional
holly and ivy are used by the bundle
and branch, with scented blue spruce
and Scots pine and their harvest
of fir cones. The metallic blue-black
berries of *Viburnum tinus* have become
a winter staple, grown for us by our
lovely Italian suppliers. As Christmas
draws near, mistletoe is added to our
arrangements, and early hellebores start
to make their way into our homes.

This natural scented wreath has a base of pine onto which a swirling frame of birch has been placed. Colorful satin ribbon has been woven into the round foliage frame and then groups of chili peppers, fir cones, and dried lotus seedheads have been added. Heavily wired dried oranges and lengths of cinnamon add to the sensual fragrance.

what winter
means to me

Winter is a time of fantasy and tradition. The introspective nature of the weather causes us to ritually explore sensations that are familiar and comforting, with a huge dash of make-believe to keep it all magical and inventive. Although the fashions come and go each year, there are always a lot of recurring themes for the winter. Traditions play an important part in our thinking and decorating at this time of year. One strong influence in the wintertime is to create a great indoor scent that evokes past cozy days and evenings. Certain foliages, spices, and seedheads provoke vivid memories. Favorites are blue pine, Scots fir, rosemary, cinnamon, oranges, star anise, and eucalyptus.

Twigs and vines, which may be overlooked at other times of the year, take central stage, and now is the time to use as many accessories are you like! For advent and the lead-up to Christmas, I like to make my arrangements natural and use principally foliage. It is quite astonishing how a simple arrangement of foliage can sometimes be more arresting than a group of flowers. When I am using foliage, I often group the material more than I would with flowers, and it is in winter that I may use more variegated plants than at any other time in the year because they do not generally complement my bold use of color.

Many winter decorations require layering, and the process seems very similar to an artist preparing a painting. At first the artist will work on the frame and the canvas and then prepare the background. This will build up with layers of paint until the artist is happy with the end result. Most winter decorations are wreaths or garlands that have a green foliage base onto which layers of accessories are added. Some may be added to give movement, while others will be chosen for their color and scent. Winter decorations need to be rich and sumptuous in their appearance, to look tactile and invite the eye with their textures. Just as we appreciate plants in winter and embrace their shape and structure, our winter decorations mirror this seasonal change. Christmas decorations need to be inviting, to evoke a sense of welcome and delight!

gift bouquets

Whenever I am planning combinations of flowers for mixed bouquets, I consider the colors, the textures, and, of course, the longevity of the flowers. The best way to choose a successful flower color combination is to study flowers in their natural habitat or in a garden. Red, yellow, and green may not be a hit if you study color theory, but study the landscape and you will know that they work very well. They make a vibrant, striking yet complementary color theme. In the winter we naturally deviate to richer and warmer colors for comfort, and most holiday schemes seem to be divided into a mix of these

tones and the devotees of the purist white Christmas. Whether that is mixed with gold or silver is largely down to personal taste and, of course, fashion!

Whenever you are selecting the materials for a hand-tied bouquet, I would recommend that you start with a selection of 25 to 35 stems, including foliage. Usually foliage will be around a third of the bouquet, and I prefer to use at least three different types, usually with some berries, so *Hedera*, *Viburnum* and *Ilex* varieties are my favorite. I also love to use flowering fillers, and at this time of year the best for short bouquets and tight arrangements is skimmia.

opposite Bright color combinations need to be blended together by the addition of dark green glossy leaves, such as rhododendron, and also here the burgundy *Photinia* 'Red Robin' leaves. All the flowers in this bouquet have very strong shapes, so they all have equal visual presence. Red 'Tropical' anthuriums mix well with 'Grand Prix' roses. Pincushion proteas (*Leucospermum cordifolium*) add texture; black-eyed gerberas add light.

this page A perennial favorite of the gardener and also the flower arranger is white. Having retailed flowers for a couple of decades, I can safely say that white is the safe option when sending flowers and by far the most popular. Chunky ornamental kales, 'Avalanche+' roses, and white *Cymbidium* orchids are softened with the addition of lilac and ruscus. Jasmine and stephanotis make this a fabulously scented combination.

classic leaf wreath

A SIMPLE RING COVERED IN EVERGREEN LEAVES ALWAYS LOOKS
SMART AND SOPHISTICATED AND IT SUITS TRADITIONAL HOMES
JUST AS WELL AS CONTEMPORARY INTERIORS

you will need

- a bag of sphagnum moss
- a 14-inch wire wreath ring
- a reel of strong wire
- a pair of florist scissors
- glossy long leaves
  such as laurel (camellia,
  rhododendron, or magnolia
  also work well)
- some German pins or
  heavy stub wire

1 Tease the moss with your fingers to add air and remove any foreign bodies from the forest floor such as cones, insects, and bark. When it is clean, bind the moss onto the frame in handfuls with the reel wire until you have completed the circle.

2 The completed moss ring will look shaggy, and so it is a good idea to snip off any loose ends and neaten the ring. It should be quite damp at this stage, holding enough moisture to keep the foliage fresh. If it is dry, submerge the ring in a sink or spray it thoroughly to give it moisture. This will help to preserve the life of the cut leaves.

3 Pin the leaves around the moss frame, making sure they are all in the same direction and covering over the first rows of pins as you work, so that none of the wiring will be visible.

this page Glued bark from a palm tree has been attached onto a straw and wire frame to make this wreath. The *Dendrobium* orchid heads have been hot glued to the dry frame to create a dramatic contrast of color and texture. Well-conditioned, the orchids will last 48 hours if left in a cool spot.

left This square wreath is very easy to make, but can be time consuming. After you have created the frame, which we usually make with sphagnum moss, we then bind over the moss with a cheap ribbon to match the color of our chosen fruits—in this case cranberries. Then the simple but laborious process of pinning in the fruits can begin. We usually use pearl-headed pins, which can be bought in many colors. Small crab apples can be used in the same way, or even small berries if you have the inclination and the patience!

festive home

AS A FLORAL DESIGNER I AM SPOILED BY THE FABULOUS FLOWERS AND FOLIAGES ON OFFER AT CHRISTMAS

But nothing gives more pleasure than taking the clippers around the garden and making some simple decoration or picking some evergreens and some fallen cones. Add a few candles and you have got a decoration that wows them year after year! I often deliberately pick a slightly larger Christmas tree than I need and then I can use a couple of branches from the bottom for my decorations. Everything else I can find in my garden, except a few stems of the heavily laden berries of *Ilex* that the clever Dutch growers manage to produce each year.

The other commercially grown evergreen I am mad about is skimmia. Cut branches are never very long, as the plant has a compact habitat, and it usually commands a reasonable price, making it unsuitable for budget collections. Do as I have in my garden—wherever I have an uninteresting space, I have added the odd plant so I always have a little to cut in the winter months. The red varieties such as *Skimmia japonica* 'Ruby King,' 'Rubinetta,' and 'Pink Panther' are great with rich combinations, and the white varieties *Skimmia* x *confusa* 'Kew Green' or *S. japonica* 'Emerald King' are popular and available though the Dutch auctions.

this page For advent I like to make a round table ring using a floral foam ring and evergreens from my garden so that the ring will last for the whole month, and we will be able to light a new candle each Sunday night for dinner. This tradition is common in Northern Europe and traditionally these advent wreaths are hung from the ceiling.

It is also at this time of year that I often turn for my inspiration to the fruit and vegetable markets. Many flowers are expensive and can be sometimes quite weak, and so I can find texture and color from adding fruits and vegetables to my arrangements. One of my favorites, which we revisit every winter, is the humble cranberry. Cranberries are a unique fruit and are always part of my Christmas dinner as well as the decoration. Their cultivation is quite fascinating, because they can grow and survive only under a very special combination of factors. Cranberries grow on low-lying vines in beds layered with sand, peat, gravel and clay. These beds are commonly known as bogs or marshes and were originally created by huge glaciers. Their growing season extends from April to November. The greatest producers of cranberries are the North Americans and this is largely confined to the Eastern Board around the state of Massachusetts. This American cranberry is officially known as *Vaccinium macrocarpon*. The European cranberry is most popularly found in Finland, where it is famously used in jams, puddings and drinks. Known as *Vaccinium oxycoccus*, this species is smaller and so used less in floral decoration.

left These festive letters have been fashioned out of dogwood and then bound with reel wire. Onto the frames we have then added branches of golden and red holly berries. Brightly toned variegated ivy leaves add more color to the combination.

For centuries, the focus at this time of year has been on the *Ilex* and *Hedera* genera, and as the Christmas Carol says, "When they are both full grown, Of all the trees in the woods, The holly bears the crown!" Majestic stems of *Ilex* berries, some at least a yard long in bright "red as any blood" and the subtler and more exclusive shades of yellow and peach play the supporting role to stately amaryllis or armfuls of winter foliages. Much European design is so fascinated by seasonal berries that they have found themselves into many intricate designs, being wired or threaded onto grasses. There is an *Ilex* berry

for every taste. *I. verticillata* 'Oosterwijk' with its Dutch name is the red-fruited cultivar that is very popular in Europe for the production of cut branches which hold their color and berries, and make an invaluable long-lasting contribution to so many flower arrangements at this time of year.

For those looking for something a bit different, try *Ilex verticillata* 'Golden Verboom'—its gold berries lighten with age. Another attractive variation is 'Oudijk's Orange.' This beauty has bright pinkish-orange fruit that lighten over time. Its berry-laden branches are very arresting, although a bit nontraditional.

left A birch twig wreath has been created by binding together four lengths of birch and then adding groups of wrapped presents. *Cymbidium* orchid heads have been placed in small vials of water that have been glued onto the frame. The orchids will last about a week on this frame in cool conditions.

seasonal wreath ideas

The most fantastic thing about Christmas is that the only thing you are limited by is your imagination to make something from nothing! Your base can be a twig wreath, a straw ring or a man-made wreath from polystyrene or floral foam. Whatever your scheme your desires are possible with a little wire and glue to decorate your seasonal wreath with just about anything.

The rules are very simple: heavy things are best wired; squishy natural items such as fruit are also best wired; ribbons and fabric items are usually anchored better by the use of wire; dried or hard goods are best "hot glued," and pretty much all the rest may generally be glued. There are several products on the market, and you can find these in floral sundries and craft shops or on Internet sites. Although I am generally not a fan of the glue gun or pot, I do concede at this time of the year that it is the best tool, and so it is worth investing in a good heavy-duty hot-melt glue gun. The truth is that hot glue generally sticks to anything because the glue congeals after it has reached a certain heat, when it is pushed through the glue gun. It is possible to acquire low melt versions that are generally kinder to plant material, but personally I think that if you are using a glue gun you might as well use a high-melt version, because if the plant material is soft or fragile it is best to wire it using the traditional methods. Using a glue gun is more time efficient, but the problem is that the fix may not be so permanent, so you may find that you need to repair your item occasionally.

opposite, above left Using different textures, some artificial and some natural, on blue spruce has created this monochromatic wreath. The circular movement of the ribbon helps to make this look more harmonious.

opposite, above right A six-pointed star shape has been made using a wire frame with a background of bay foliage. Artichokes, cones, and apples have been wired into the frame. A round Christmas ball in the center accentuates this shape.

opposite, below left Contrasting colors have been placed in groups to make this heavily decorative wreath.

opposite, below right This keyhole-shaped wreath uses lots of three-dimensional shapes to create a rich, jewel-like appearance.

Ring the changes for winter color and sparkle in a variety of shapes

To create a lavish wreath, you need to layer on lots of decorations. A few coatings of spray paint can transform any item to match your theme. In recent years more and more decorative items find their way to the Dutch flower auctions and so the choice for the professional florist is immense.

you will need

- a bag of sphagnum moss
- a 14-inch wire wreath ring
- a bunch of blue pine
- a pair of heavy florist scissors
- a reel of strong wire
- a selection of long strong wires
- a reel of ribbon
- 10 small apples
- 3 large and 10 small fir cones
- a bunch of mistletoe
- 5 dried limes and 10 orange slices
- a pack of long cinnamon
- a bunch of larch twigs
- a bunch of holly sprigs

1 Before you can start to use sphagnum moss, you need to tease it, to give it some air and make it less compact, and to remove any foreign bodies such as bark, twigs, insects, and so on. Once it has been cleaned it can be bound onto a wire wreath frame using heavy reel wire. Attach the wire and bind over and under the wire frame.

2 Once the ring of moss has been completed, tidy it by trimming with the scissors, and then begin to add the base of foliage. It is easier if you bind the foliage onto the frame rather than wire each individual sprig. Use three pieces for each section of the ring—one pointing inward, one outward, and one for the central area.

3 Next you need to wire all your decorations with a heavy stub wire so that you can place them into the frame. For the cones, apples, dried limes, and orange slices, place a wire through the base of the item and then bind together the two lengths of wire to produce a stem that you can place into the moss.

4 Wire the decorations and holly sprigs in groups onto the frame and then add some sprigs of larch to encircle the wreath and give it some movement. Next, take the length of ribbon and pin it around the wreath so that it looks as though it is weaving in and out from the center to the edge.

spiced ring
THIS TIGHTLY PACKED WREATH IS THE EPITOME
OF A TRADITIONAL CHRISTMAS

Christmas tables

As the iconic magazine editor Diana Vreeland said, "Pink is the navy blue of India," and red and white are certainly the customary colors of Christmas. Despite the fashions and trends of each year the overwhelming color choices for Christmas remain the same, with a touch of gold or silver. Each year the rise in prices at the Dutch auctions for these two shades, with red always clearly winning the Christmas poll, is testament to our adherence to traditional values for the holiday season. I guess part of the reason for this is we visit all these traditions just once a year, and the pressure to get it just right and to fulfill the expectations of all, mean that we all err on the side of comfort. Christmas is not a time to try out new recipes or decorations, but to re-present the familiar, the traditional, and even the predictable!

By the time I come to plan my own Christmas, I am desperate for a new look, and a color that departs from the majority of decorations we have been producing in our workshops. Last year it was all green and white, but with a very acid citrus theme and a lot of fragrance. This year I was inspired by these new shocking pink containers and so mixed pink with gold for a very rich combination. Inspired by the fabrics and artwork of India, the Moroccan tea glasses used as votives and as tiny vases add to the exotic feel of this table setting.

opposite, far left The process of coloring and flocking natural stems and seedheads has become more prevalent in recent years, and one of the most popular are *Mitsumata* twigs. Here their vivid color complements the naturally brightly colored gerberas.

opposite, center Moroccan tea hold small bouquets for individual place settings.

opposite, right A napkin tie of a rose with dried orange slices and artificial gold decoration complements the scheme.

this page Three hand-tied bouquets of 'Aqua!', 'Black Baccara,' and 'Colandro' roses are mixed with bunches of red skimmia to form the main centerpiece.

you will need

- a round metal candle sconce with some chains for hanging
- a reel of heavy florist wire
- several lengths of long green trailing ivy
- a bunch of larch stems
- 10 stems of *Hypericum* berries
- 20 burgundy carnations
- 5 stems of hanging green amaranthus
- 8 long taper candles

1 Attach your reel wire to the metal ring. Completely cover the base of the frame by binding the larch stems and the ivy around the wreath using the reel wire. Allow some of the twiggy pieces of larch to stick out so that they give the ring some movement.

2 Continue binding loosely around the ring with your reel wire and add the *Hypericum* that has been cut and prepared into lengths of around 2 inches. You can attach small vials of water to the plant material at this point if you require the decoration to last a long time.

3 At this stage it is best to work on the item while it is hanging so that you can view it from all directions. Finally, add groups of carnations and hanging green amaranthus so that they are at different heights and depths around the ring. Make sure that the ring looks good viewed from beneath as well as from the top. Finally, fix the candles into the holders. Mist the foliage or submerge the wreath overnight to keep it fresh.

hanging candelabra
WREATHS ARE VERY VERSATILE AND MAKE VERY PRETTY
DECORATIONS SUSPENDED ON CHAINS OR RIBBONS

New Year's Eve party

Rather than battle with the crowds out and about on New Year's Eve, I prefer to spend the occasion at home, celebrating with friends and family. The tradition of staying up until midnight to mark the transition of the old year into the new one dictates that this is going to be a lengthy session, so it is an event for which it is worth making an effort on the decoration front.

After the excesses of Christmas I sometimes like to create a cool-looking theme for a New Year's Eve dinner, such as this elegant white scheme. In deference to the arrival of the new year, with its feelings of renewal and rejuvenation, I often incorporate living plant material as an indication that the new growing season is not too far away now. Bulbs, which give that first hint of spring-like activity when they start to poke their heads above frozen winter soil in the garden, are now readily available in potted form in the weeks leading up to Christmas, and so they are ideal choices. Delicate snowdrops work well, as do the hyacinths and narcissi I have used here.

left This hyacinth bulb has been especially treated so that it will bloom early. Remove it from its pot and gently wash all the soil off the roots before placing it on top of a clear glass so that the roots form part of the display. A tiny white Christmas tree bauble sits on the rim to echo the central display.

this page and left I love the graphic quality of simple twig wreaths painted white; these can easily be bought already made. I used a bowl-shaped one as a centerpiece, filling the middle with pots of fragrant paperwhite narcissi overlaid with trailing jasmine and groups of small, shiny pearl baubles. Silver lanterns and more jasmine trails continue the theme on the rest of the table.

naming parties

WHETHER AN INTIMATE FAMILY GATHERING OR A MORE LAVISH EVENT, FLOWERS HELP TO MARK THE OCCASION

In an increasingly secular and multicultural society where marriages have become ever more fragile, a naming ceremony followed by a party are a way of celebrating without causing any offense to race or religion. As families relocate for work, moving from city to city and country to country, there is something reassuring about a naming ceremony. Whichever type you choose, it is a very special way of celebrating the birth of your child and welcoming the new arrival or addition into the family and the wider community. It is also ideally suited to welcome an older child into the family, particularly if there has not been a celebration previously. It is the perfect way to bond a family and celebrate an adoption or to embrace stepchildren into a new family.

It's also an opportunity to declare before family and friends your promises to be as good a parent as you can, and for adult friends or relatives to confirm their special relationship with your child. Usually sponsors are called upon to look out for the individual as they pledge their love and support for the child's future development. This back-up infrastructure of chosen adults cements relationships as it establishes to old friends that you want to keep them in your life as your children grow. As for the flowers for the party, well, they are easier to choose than your friends, because certain flowers do suit the occasion more! The botanical study of flowers splits inflorescent types that really are determined by their structure and appearance. Umbrella shapes such as Queen Anne's lace and fennel are very fragile and delicate. Some airy shapes such as *Gypsophila* and saponica also work very well. Children are very drawn themselves to the familiar round and flat formed flowers such as daisies, anemones, and poppies, and less so to spathe shapes such as calla lilies and the waxy anthurium.

christening themes

this page A small foam ring surrounds a storm lantern. The base of flowering *Viburnum tinus* has been decorated with guelder roses, large 'Avalanche+' rose heads, and delicate hellebores.

Christening or baptism celebrations are both religious affairs. Baptism is not unique to Christianity and usually involves a person being anointed by holy water as a symbol of protection. A Christening establishes both the naming of an individual child and his or her dedication to God and the Christian faith.

Following a short church service a lunch or a tea may be served, with white being overwhelmingly the color of choice because of its association with purity. It is symbolic of the promises the godparents assembled around the font will make "to renounce the devil and all his works, believing in God's Holy Word and never breaking the Ten Commandments." White flowers have long been associated with the Virgin Mary and have been included in many historic art works depicting the Madonna. A white lily is symbolic of purity and sweetness and is often associated with children or young women. Daisies are another flower that has a long association with youth and symbolizes purity and youth. White flowers also seem a perfect choice to decorate the celebrations of a birth or a young child.

this page Shot glasses in a ring make a simple table center when filled with snowdrops and sprigs of jasmine. Twisted decorative florist wire has been gently wound around the stems for added visual interest.

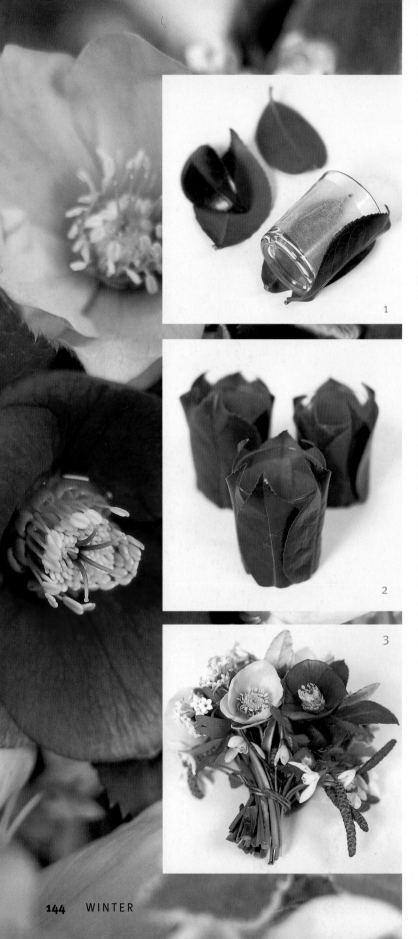

you will need

- 3 glass votives
- a roll of double-sided tape
- 2 branches of laurel
- 6 stems of variegated pittosporum
- a bunch of snowdrops
- a bunch of hellebores
- 3 stems of catkins
- a bunch of aconites
- 6 stems of *Viburnum* x *bodnantense*
- florist string for tying

christening table center

DELICATE MINIATURE BOUQUETS MAKE APPROPRIATE DECORATIONS FOR BABY CELEBRATIONS

1 First place some double-sided tape all around the glasses. Stick some laurel leaves all around the edge of the glass votives in an upright fashion, overlapping them slightly.

2 Trim the bottom off the leaves so they are flush with the glass and then fill the glass with water. It is always a good idea to add some flower food, particularly for fragile cut-garden flowers such as the ones used here.

3 Trim the lower foliage from the stems of the flowers and foliages, cut them to the same length and then hand-tie into small posies. Secure them with florist string. Once tied, cut the stems again to fit snugly into the leafed pots.

Valentines are sent each year worldwide, making the day the second largest card-sending holiday of the year, trailing only behind Christmas!

On February 14th the British spend around £30 million on flowers and plants, 99 per cent of which is spent on flowers. Nine million of this figure is spend more specifically on red roses and it is calculated that men buy around 90 per cent of the day's flowers! The majority of roses sold in the world on that day are grown and produced in Colombia, Ecuador, Holland, India, Israel, Kenya, Zimbabwe, Ethiopia, and other smaller flower-producing countries. Over 50 million roses are traded on this one day. Now that the Russians and the Japanese are avid buyers of roses, there is a huge global demand for this one product in a very short time frame, which inevitably causes supply problems and consequently higher prices than during the rest of the year. Demand simply outstrips supply and every year the flower industry receives bad press because of the inevitable hike in prices. However, despite this cynicism, it never ceases to amaze me that the demand stays very focused on the traditional dozen red roses, and the purchasing pattern is always to leave it to the last minute! Year after year we have analyzed our sales figures, which conclude that the hour that trade is most buoyant is the hour after work on the day itself, before customers make their way home or to their romantic dinner!

Valentine's Day

THIS IS THE TRADITIONAL DAY ON WHICH LOVERS EXPRESS THEIR LOVE FOR ONE ANOTHER BY SENDING VALENTINE'S CARDS OR FLOWERS, OR OFFERING OTHER GIFTS

St. Valentine's Day is celebrated on February 14th each year in Europe and the U.S. It would seem that this celebration takes its name from early Christian martyrs named Valentine. The day appears to have become linked with romantic themes some time in the middle ages, as we know from the writings of Geoffrey Chaucer, when courtly love flourished.

Modern day Valentine symbols include anything heart-shaped or associations with the winged Cupid! Since the nineteenth century, handwritten notes have largely given way to mass-produced greeting cards. The sending of Valentine's cards became a fashion in Victorian Britain. This trend spread first to America, but has now caught on all over the world and now not only causes a huge upward spiraling of the flower market worldwide, but also a bulge in the stationery industry, which estimates that approximately one billion

this page A heart-shaped frame has been created from dogwood and then skimmia, *Ranunculus*, tulips, *Cymbidium* orchids, and bunches of *Muscari* added. Coils of bright pink metallic wire add extra sparkle.

opposite, above Pink and white are second in line—albeit a long way down the pecking order—of choice after red in the popularity stakes. Here lengths of black bamboo wired onto ornamental florists' reel wire encircle 'Aqua!' roses. This has then been placed onto a metal bouquet frame to help distribute the weight.

opposite, below A twig frame of flexible willow has been fashioned into a heart, before the sap rises in early spring. Onto this heart feathers and faux butterflies, lengths of decorative pearls, and *Cymbidium* orchid heads have been wired.

below Great alternatives to roses for Valentine's Day are the heart-shaped red anthuriums. Here they are arranged with the green *Anthurium crystallinum* with its beautiful raised vein markings in a circular group of three zinc moon vases. Often hugely underrated, these sexy flowers are incredibly long lasting and a much better value than the sweetest rose!

opposite, left Amaryllis makes another good choice for Valentine's Day and particularly a gift for a male Valentine. Tying 'Red Lion' amaryllis with black rope, then placing on a pin holder in a glass dish filled with a covering of polished black stones, created this living topiary.

opposite, right These polished copper heart-shaped stands were made for me by a group of talented German florists trading as Belle Art. I love to use them for weddings around Valentine's Day; the shorter ones make excellent table decorations while the taller are great for reception areas. Exuberantly and extravagantly filled with long tall gloriosa lilies and garlanded with the short gloriosa, this would certainly woo anyone in the floral trade!

love in the air

The overwhelming majority of Valentine purchasers are men—in 24 hours of serving in my flower store on Oxford Street in London on February 13th and 14th this year, I did not serve one woman! Maybe that is because women are more organized and do not leave it to the last minute, or perhaps they buy flowers more confidently by telephone or on the Internet. However, we do send a tiny percentage of flowers on Valentine's Day to men from women acting as modern-day cupids. Apart from tropical flowers such as anthuriums or gingers, I often recommend strong masculine-style flowers such as amaryllis or calla lilies. Failing that, if you are looking for something to woo a hot-blooded male, go for something unusual such as gloriosa or *Sandersonia*, or a classic flower such as tulips. As tulips are in season and therefore relatively inexpensive in February, and are available in over a hundred varieties, you must be able to find one to suit the man in your life!

you will need:

- 20 'Grand Prix' roses
- 20 'Cool Water' roses
- a bunch of camellia foliage
- a bunch of green broom
- a bunch of thin red Iranian dogwood
- a reel of florist wire
- a pair of florist scissors

1 First make a wreath by binding the broom and thin Iranian dogwood together with heavy reel wire. Carry on binding it all together until you have a neat round frame about 10 inches in diameter.

2 Next, clean the stems of roses so that they have no foliage and also remove any thorns from the stems so that they are less painful for you to handle. Next start to create a spiralled bouquet, incorporating all the roses and interspersing the colors. Edge with neat sprigs of camellia foliage.

3 Place the bouquet into the middle of the wreath and then take some longer pieces of broom and weave them around the bouquet looping them above the height of the flower heads. Take care to make sure that one end is able to drink water among the rose stems.

Valentine bouquet

ROSES REMAIN THE FIRST CHOICE FOR MANY ROMANTICS, AND
IN THIS BOUQUET THEY ARE GIVEN A CONTEMPORARY TWIST

seasonal flower directory

spring

Acacia There are many hybrids of mimosa that are available from December to March. These fluffy yellow flowers have a great scent and can be used in hand-tied bouquets as well as rings.

Anemone These beautiful jewel-colored flowers are heavy drinkers, so they are best used in hand-tied bouquets. Remember to refresh vase water frequently or keep foam very damp if arranging them in a ring. Anemones continue to grow once cut, so allow for this when creating bouquets.

Cytisus Scented broom is grown commercially in Italy and adds a wonderful fragrance to any spring arrangement. There are lots of lovely pale and pastel colors, which are much subtler than the bright yellow varieties seen growing on poor scrubland in the wild. Great for bouquets and can be used short as a filler for rings.

Freesia This is popular due to its beautiful scent. When buying, check for maturity—the main bud must be fully grown and showing color. Never leave without water, as freesias are very sensitive to dehydration. Works in both foam and water.

Hyacinthus Heavy spikes of waxy bell-shaped fragrant spring flowers in white, blue, pink, purple, peach, yellow, cream, or red which are great for hand-tied bouquets. The delicate bells are perfect for piping and wiring together. Hyacinths can be used in foam, but their heavy fleshy stems require a more skilled flower arranger.

Leucojum aestivum Nodding white flowers on strong green stems, snowflakes resemble a larger version of the treasured snowdrop. They are increasing in supply because they have a much better vase life than snowdrops and can be used in both foam and small hand-tied bouquets.

Muscari Beautiful diminutive flower that comes in blue, white, and green varieties. These can be used in planted arrangements, or as cut flowers. Their fleshy short stems make them challenging for foam work, but they can be used in rings and are popular for christenings and baby birth bouquets.

Narcissus These elegant flowers, usually yellow or white, are useful for all decorations from vase arrangements to bouquets. They can also be used in wreaths, though like hyacinths their fleshy stems require careful handling. The stems give off slime, which has an unfavorable effect on other flowers, so make sure you condition them for several hours in flower food before mixing them. The smaller-headed varieties such as 'Tête-à-tête' are great in planted arrangements.

Ranunculus My all-time favorite flower is popular in bouquets and bridal work. These beautiful flowers look their best the day before they expire, when their petals become translucent. Remove any lower foliage from the stems, as they will contaminate the water.

Syringa Varieties of lilac are available from winter through to early summer. These branches of large trusses of flowers, some with fragrance, are now available in varying shades of purple to white. Lilacs are ideal for hand-tied bouquets and can be used in wreaths. I am in love with some of the new cream varieties and dusty pink colors that have a very romantic faded look to them.

Salix Willow stems are malleable in the spring and are ideal to line glass containers horizontally or vertically. They can also be used in tall bouquets with lilies or roses and other woody spring flowers.

Tulipa Versatile flower in a range of forms to suit all tastes. Good for hand-tied bouquetss and vases. Remember the tulips will continue to grow in water, sometimes as much as 2 inches. The long stems are great for natural displays and look particularly good in wreaths.

Viburnum tinus and V. opulus I just could not image spring without these two. The white blossom of *Viburnum tinus* is great, as are many of the other early spring varieties, but *Viburnum opulus* 'Roseum' is wonderful at supporting other flowers and making the whole combination improve by the vibrant green it brings to the design. These balls of spring bring a zingy acid tone that freshens and lifts the effect of adjacent flowers and foliage. Deserves an Oscar for its supporting role!

Viola Violets come from a massive family and they are represented in the wild all over the world—they are an historical and hugely emotive flower. Some varieties have a scent and Italy has been one of the main producers. They are fantastic for small bouquets, napkins ties, and in wedding work. You could make a wreath from them but they would have to be pinned into the foam or moss in bunches. They are more likely to be used in sympathy wreaths because of their connotations as flowers of remembrance, which have been immortalized forever in the words of Shakespeare.

Zantedeschia Known as the calla or arum lily, these are very versatile flowers, which are useful for all aspects of flower arranging. They are grown to be plentiful in spring and have for ages been a staple for Easter church decoration.

summer

Agapanthus Tall blue or white architectural flower which is very useful for line bouquets or massed together. Heads made an interesting texture in wreaths and are long lasting.

Alchemilla mollis An invaluable filler plant for bouquets and rings, with textural fluffy flower heads in vibrant acid green.

Asclepias These branched flowers are great fillers for bouquets and can also be used in summer ring arrangements. I love the big orange star-shaped heads of the 'Beatrix,' variety and the dusty pink *A incarnata* 'Cinderella' in summer wedding work.

Astilbe Pretty, fluffy, and delicate, astilbe are great for summer arrangements, but they dry out very quickly so are best in water rather than foam.

Astrantia These beautiful star-shaped flowers in red, pink, and white are perfect for hand-tied bouquets. They are a great support act for summer focal flowers. Like astilbe, this flower has delicate stems and prefers water to foam.

Campanula Great for summer vases and large bouquet arrangements. The multi-headed stem survives better in water than in florist foam and should never be allowed to dry out.

Cosmos Graceful, disk-shaped summer flowers, available in pink, white and deep red. Chocolate *Cosmos astrosanginus*, in particular, is a striking bridal flower, with the subtle aroma of its namesake. Great in small bouquets and as napkin decorations, but too delicate for rings or large wreaths.

Dahlia Dahlias are the most gorgeous members of the daisy family, available from midspring to early winter, with supply peaking between midsummer and midautumn. Dahlias add an interesting textual interest to hand-tied bouquets and vase arrangements, but are also fantastic in wreaths, where their diverse shapes and colors can be used to great advantage.

Delphinium The smaller varieties are great for large hand-tied bouquets and vases, while the hybrids are excellent for large arrangements and bridal work. The shorter varieties are less expensive and can be cut down to use in wreaths for their amazing colors.

Eryngium Great for flower arrangements and also for bridal work. Their vase life ranges from 12 to 16 days, maybe longer in cool conditions.

Gerbera Useful for all aspects of floristry. Fantastic for hand-tied bouquets, particularly the smaller Germini varieties, while the large heads are excellent fillers for table wreaths. Avoid touching flower heads, which are easily damaged, and particularly sensitive to bacteria, so make sure that the vase and water are clean.

Gloriosa Short-stemmed varietes are useful for napkin ties while the longer trailing stems are great in bouquets and larger displays. This fragile flower is often shipped in inflated plastic bags to avoid damage. Stunning two-tone flowers are usually bright scarlet with a yellow edge.

Helianthus Sunflowers, some of monumental size, with golden-yellow petals radiating from large, usually dark centers, are great in hand-tied bouquets and rings.

Iris Useful for bouquets and they make an interesting flower for vegetative or natural designs. Blue, yellow, and white varieties are available, but they don't have great stamina so try to arrange them in water unless you are using them for a particular special event.

Lathyrus Good for simple vase arrangements and a popular choice for weddings because of their delicacy. Sweet peas are very fragrant, and although they prefer to be in water rather than in foam, the commercially grown varieties which have been post-harvest treated last surprisingly long in comparison with those picked from your garden. Always use flower food.

Lilium Lilies are long lasting and adored for their scent. It is advisable to remove the anthers to prevent pollen staining the flowers, surfaces, or clothing. Single heads are great in rings and wedding arrangements and stems can be used in large bouquets. Be careful using in wreaths because they have an association with funerals.

Matthiola Short lived but beautifully scented, these flowers are great for hand-tied bouquets and can be used in wreaths, especially vegetative ones, where there is the chance to use its length.

Paeonia Peonies are prized for all kinds of floristry and flower arranging. Popular for summer weddings—depending on the variety, they range from slightly fragrant to heavily scented.

Phalaenopsis Good for wedding bouquets, displaying in single vases and in decorative floristry, these orchids are excellent as pot plants. Flaccid flowers can be refreshed by submerging them in lukewarm water.

Rosa The most popular flower in the industry, due to its wide variation in color and size. Vase life is generally from 8 to 20 days if placed in water with flower food. Roses can be used in all area of floristry and are an all-year staple in hand-tied bouquets and wreaths.

Scabiosa Open, ruffled flowers in varied colors of blue, mauve, crimson, or white, These summer flower looks stunning in hand-tied bouquets, giving a "country garden" feel to rings.

fall

Brassica oleracea Acephala Group The season of the ornamental kale has been widely extended as the popularity of this long lasting chunky headed "flower" has continued to grow. This rosette shaped flower head is great for bouquets and also in wreaths and it comes in green, white, and purple.

Callicarpa bodinieri Excellent for vase arrangements and great for autumn weddings. The short season of this plant makes it an annual treat and the color of the berries is often a talking point. Can be used in bowls with floating candles.

Celosia The rich vivid colors of celosia and their unusual texture provide interest in hand-tied bouquets and rings. I prefer the Cristata Group with the textural round heads to the pointed Plumosa Group, but I adore the colors of both. Place in a clean vase with cut-flower food for the longest life. Avoid fluctuations in temperature.

Chrysanthemum Chrysanthemums are extremely versatile and long lasting. Their vase life is generally from 10 to 14 days, though some varieties will last as long as 3 weeks! They do very well in rings, although they have connotations of being a funeral flower so avoid using them en masse. The small Santini varieties have their heads at the same level and were specifically developed for the hand-tied market. Currently the standard "bloom" heads are having a revival and are great massed or used in bouquets.

Cotinus coggygria Rich dark foliage, which adds depth to arrangements and helps balance bright flower combinations. It also works well with dark reds and burgundy and is a personal favorite of mine. I also love the aromatic woody scent.

Fagus Deep rust-colored autumn foliage which mixes well with a host of bright orange flowers and fruits for a seasonal arrangement. I love to use the copper beech colors and we use a lot of beech from Italy that is treated with a substance so that the leaves last several months. This stabilized beech is great for long-lasting wreaths.

Hypericum Shiny berries which add texture and interest to arrangements, varying in color from brown, green, red, yellow, to orange. Once a fall treasure, it is now a very hard working plant available 52 weeks of the year—invaluable and always on the stock list. Thanks to an increasing number of varieties we still love it.

Leucospermum Very useful for hand-tieds and arrangements, these flowers are excellent for contract work because of their longevity in water and even in foam. They are available in orange and yellow all year. Fall was traditionally a good time for them and it is during this period that different varieties are available.

Photinia The 'Red Robin' foliage is great for contrasting with brightly colored flowers and fall is traditionally its best time, although its popularity means that its season is extending as a commercially grown cut flower. I am also very fond of the darker 'Purple Peter' variety and I love to cut it from my own garden when it flowers.

Physalis Popular for Halloween. The orange lanterns also make cheerful dried flowers and can last up to two years. The tall stems can be used in bouquets and the lanterns wired into wreaths. The leaves wither, but the seedheads last for months.

Quercus Rusty brown autumn foliage which mixes well with burgundy, brown, plum, and deep-red flowers in arrangements. Many varieties are popular but the so-called American oaks, *Quercus palustris* and *Quercus rubra* are great for flower arrangements. We also love to use these branches when they have been treated like stablized beech so that they last longer.

Rosa Rosehip add texture and a seasonal feel to arrangements. Add interest to containers by creating a collar around a bouquet and placing it into a cylindrical vase, or mix with foliage in all arrangements. The season for hips is increasing and their appeal growing. Look out for 'Sensational Fantasy' and 'Amazing Fantasy' as interesting fillers for autumn arrangements.

Rubus fruiticosus Blackberries are lovely to use in hand-tied bouquets as they give a wild and natural look to brash fall flower such as dahlias. I am particularly grateful to the hybridizers who have come up with *R. laciniatus* 'Thornless Evergreen' as this one has none of the spiteful thorns found on the hedgerow plants.

Sandersonia This looks like a supermodel version of *Physalis*, with delicate lanterns on a wispy green stem. Available from spring to fall commercially, this plant originates from Africa. Too delicate to be much use in rings, this fragile beauty adds to bouquets and hand-tieds.

Sedum There are lots of lovely varieties of this long-lasting and versatile flower head. In the early part of fall it is fun to use green and I like to use the branches heads of 'Matrona' rather than some of the larger denser heads, which can be too dominant against other flower heads.

Symphoricarpos Snowberries used to grow wild along railway embankments when I was small—they were fun to find and pop on autumnal walks! Now their small pink, blush, or white waxy berries are the height of fashion. This unusual foliage adds shape and texture to arrangements and is fantastic for wedding arrangements.

winter

Cymbidium Good for weddings and corporate work and—because they are extravagant and symbolize love—popular for Valentine's Day. Also, a good long-lasting flower for the festive season.

Eucalyptus Although you can get eucalyptus all year round, the flowering and fruiting varieties are most useful in winter. I like to use *Eucalyptus robusta* for its flowers and *Eucalyptus globulus* for its gray scented seedheads. These are highly aromatic, which can border on the unpleasant, so do not keep for too long. Useful in all types of floristry.

Euphorbia fulgens Arching member of the huge *Euphorbia* family, whose famous family member the poinsettia is synonymous with Christmas despite being a tropical flower! These long-stemmed branches are most useful for bouquets but can be cut down to give color—of which it comes in a dozen or so shades—to rings. Watch out for the white sap as it is an irritant to the skin.

Hedera The holly and the ivy are essential at this time of year. Ivy in all its forms and varieties is an essential at our workshop and bunches of berried ivies are used in bouquets and wreaths all winter.

Helleborus *Helleborus niger* is the so-called Christmas rose that is depicted on masses of Christmas cards. Later flowering varieties are known as Lenten roses as they flower nearer Easter. The first flowers are brought on for Christmas by our suppliers in Italy and appear in small paper-wrapped bouquets in later November and early December. The supply goes on well into spring and even till the beginning of May. Great in small bouquets and wreaths.

Hibiscus Most of us get to see hibiscus flowers and humming birds when enjoying a hot break if we are lucky. However the fruit of *Hibiscus trionum*, which is from the Mediterranean, is great for festive hand-tied bouquets and wreaths. Its bright red color and interesting shape make it an unusual addition to designs, especially when other material is scarce.

Hippeastrum Amaryllis are highly valued as cut flowers because of their impressive vase life. To ensure optimum blooming, remove pollen-bearing stamens and place a bamboo cane into their hollow stem to help the plant bear the weight of the flower heads when opened.

Galanthus The common snowdrops are one of the world's most loved flowers because they are among the first bulbs to flower in winter. They are not a very useful cut flower as they do not last well, and are too delicate for foam. Not to be confused with their relatives the snowflakes, *Leucojum* species, which are much larger and flower in the spring.

Garrya elliptica Gray foliage from this plant, and especially its male and female catkins, which appear from winter to early summer, make this a lovely textural filler for winter bouquets and rings.

Ilex The bushy green holly forms are great for wreaths and the tall leafless stems are great for large bouquets or cut down into small bouquets. The common red-berried varieties are available from later autumn to Christmas, with some very special yellow or peach varieties appearing at the peak of the festive season when they fetch high prices.

Jasmininum nudiflorum The early flowering yellow jasmine is a winter treat. I think of *Jasminum officinale* as being an indoor pot plant for the winter and always have a few around my home at Christmas. So I have included jasmine here, although it really is around in some form for most of the year. Great in bouquets and rings for scent.

Ligustrum I love the black berries and use this as filler in bouquets and rings from autumn to Christmas. The scent reminds me of my grandmother, who used to have a bush in her garden. It is a semi-evergreen or deciduous shrub so the berries are on woody stems, leafless as it gets nearer to Christmas and the winter sets in.

Pinus No winter time could be without pine in its many forms and also the use of its fruit, the pine cone. Useful in all areas of floristry, but most notably in Christmas wreaths.

Primula Technically a spring plant—the name means *little first thing*—but one of the first to flower in my garden. This genus of nearly 500 species of low-growing herbs are a godsend in the bleak months after Christmas when the flower market lacks inspiration. The flowers are very sweet in small bouquets and wedding work, but the whole plant makes a cheap addition to rings in winter.

Viburnum Blue-tinged berries from viburnums add depth to arrangements. The heavily berried branch belongs to *Viburnum dentatum*, and the variety that is grown commercially in the Netherlands is called 'Inge.' It is always on our order list when it is in season because it is so useful and pretty.

Viscum album Mistletoe—a mystic plant with a complex history of folklore and an essential for winter. No home is ready for the holidays until you have hung your bouquet of mistletoe to kiss under! Also useful in hand-tied bouquets and cut short in rings. This mysterious parasitic plant in its European form is said to have fertility and life-enhancing properties.

index

Figures in italics indicate captions.

acknowledgments

At the close of another book my thank you list, as usual, is long and has included a cast of many. I am really grateful to Sarah Cuttle, my photographer, for her cheerful and talented approach to this book, and for giving so much to the project. Thanks, too, for the practical and pragmatic approach of her assistant Will. Maggie Town has waved her magic on the design of the book and has been hugely supportive of the whole team. Sian Parkhouse, too, has done a wonderful job of making sense of and editing the endless early morning emails that I have sent her, and always manages to make the impossible appear achievable—which ultimately it must be for me to be on the last page now! Thanks to Charles Miers, my American publisher, for taking another Paula Pryke book and for this time even suggesting the title, and to Jacqui Small for masterminding the whole project. Thanks also to her team who make all this possible.

Thanks to my team, most notably Sarah Laugher, who has kept me on track and contributed so much to this project and the running of my day-to-day business. Penny Mallinson has also been invaluable, and also thank you to all the team who shared their talents and worked directly on the shoots of the book: Viktor Tordai, Vilija Vaitilaite, Lynn Davis, Kate Wozniak, Estelle Montlouis, Samantha Griffiths, Heidi Bradshaw, Anita Everard, and Wendy Boileau.

A huge thank you to all the rest of the managers, floral designers, students, and drivers who have worked for me during the production of this book: Chris Sharples, Anna Hudson, Anita Kovacevic, Anne Cadle, Tania Newman, Kirsten Dalgleish, Shontelle Jepson, Ann Pochetty, Joanne Rouse, Natasha Tshoukas, Katie Cochrane, Hyunah Lee, Su Yeon Lee, Hisako Watanabe, Miranda Laraso, Gillian Munday, Laura Penny, Hayley Pryke, Miki Tanabe, Gemma Tobutt, Marianne Schmidt, Hyun Soo Lee, Karin Persson, Steve Dzingel, Jason Fielding, Rosanna Manfredi, and Phil O'Neil.

Thank you, too, to all the wholesalers who provided flowers and plants for this book and for their help with the identification and also, of course, our botanical expert Tony Lord.